BATTLE FOR NORTHUMBRIA

Battle for NORTHUMBRIA

An odyssey through
the violent history of
the turbulent border
Kingdom

John Sadler

Illustrated by James Mayer

Bridge Studios
Morpeth
Northumberland
1988

Dedicated to Ruth

First published in Great Britain in 1988

by Bridge Studios
   4B Bridge Street
   Morpeth
   Northumberland
   NE61 1NB
   Tel.: 0670 518101/519561

© John Sadler 1988
Illustrations © Bridge Studios 1988

ISBN 0 9512630 3 X

Illustrations and cover design by James Mayer.

Printed by Martin's of Berwick

Contents

Foreword

When men of strong and athletic physique were ready to challenge their equals in single combat, the writers of ballads were eager to praise their deeds; and when society was divided into rival clans a climate was created in which war was invested with glamour, and deeds of chivalry and valour held the stage.

John Sadler's well-researched story of the battlefields of Northumbria and the Scottish lowlands brings us nearer to the harsh realities of life for the great majority of the peoples who lived in those inhospitable hills where survival was marginal and existence hazardous. Northumberland had enjoyed a period of comparative calm and culture while the Romans governed England, for to the south of Hadrian's Wall the legions had kept law and order. But when the Roman Empire began to shrink the wall crumbled and economic and social order dissolved into chaos.

The Viking invaders were fierce and cruel; the Celts from Scotland were always on the lookout for rich pickings; while the Normans were by nature conquerors ruling by military occupation either directly, or through their affiliated feudal lords, who governed by strength of arms.

The Scots were a turbulent lot. They sought to compensate for the poverty of the mountain soil by pillaging their neighbour's livestock and scorching their neighbour's earth. The Black Douglas, the 'Good' Sir James, noted by contemporaries for his valour and courtesy was a past master of such tactics. War-like tribes — Maxwells, Douglas's, Kers and Elliots and Armstrongs, were constantly feuding. The astonishing thing is that following the carnage of the multitude of raids, the Scots had any energy to fight the English.

Time and again the Scots would muster their forces and draw up in solid formation armed with their pikes, and time and again the arrows of the English longbows (six arrows could be fired by one archer in one minute) cut swathes in the Scottish ranks until the border burns and rivers literally ran with blood. It ran too out of the veins of Scotland and weakened the stamina of the wounded nation.

The Douglas and Percy of the day were the popular champions of the hour and the theme of many a heroic song. On that evidence, if their generalship was defective, their courage was matchless.

It has been a long rough road from the arrows of the longbows hailing out of the sky to the threat posed by fallout from the nuclear missile of today. Is it too much to hope that at long last man will decide that there is no longer any romance or any gain in war.

Lord Home of the Hirsel K.T.

Douglas John Sadler was born and raised in the North East of England and has maintained a lifelong passion for local and military history. The turbulent years of the Anglo Scottish border wars have always been of special interest and have, to a certain extent, been neglected by historians.

Born in 1953 and educated at a local grammar school, he obtained his first degree in law at Newcastle Polytechnic and, more recently, an M.Phil. after several years as a part-time research student under the aegis of the Polytechnic of Central London. His main interests at school were history, acting and debate and he has always been interested in the re-enactment of dark age and medieval combat; he is a member of the Knights Templar.

He lives in Belsay and is married with one daughter.

The Battle Trail

Northumbria is an embattled and much fortified landscape — not unsurprisingly, the two tend to go together; harsh realities now softened by a patina of age and veneer of romance. Because large areas of the county remain undeveloped, numerous battle sites remain almost as they were; even in a city as heavily industrialised as Newcastle, substantial sections of the medieval walls survive, as, of course, do the still mighty Keep and Black Gate. The Joicey Museum contains an excellent model of the final storming by the Scots in 1644. Newburn Church, prior to the fight for the river crossing, provides the same 'long view' today — though Stella Power Station is a later addition!

The location of various battlefields is indicated by O.S. references in the text, some of which are commemorated by markers or monuments, others not. In several instances the discerning visitor can still determine who it was stood where, and look upon a landscape that would not be unfamiliar to the warrior of old.

The military road, B6318, as it approaches the descent to Chollerford from the east, passes a roadside-cross commemorating the Northumbrians' delivery from the Welsh in 635 and the site is further celebrated by St. Oswald's Chapel. The field remains more charged with atmosphere than the later Wars of the Roses' sites near Hexham. The uncompromising line of Hadrian's Wall survives and it is not hard to picture the dreadful slaughter of the rout over Fallowfield Fell.

Alnwick, though the castle is now much altered; 'classicised' in the eighteenth and re-'gothicised' in the nineteenth centuries, remains a medieval town in plan, girded by the almost palpable might and valour of the Percies. Malcolm's Cross, just to the north of the centre, bears mute witness to the final fall of Shakespeare's Canmore. Sadly, the site of William the Lion's battle is not remembered. It should be; few market towns in England can have laid low two such powerful invaders.

The bitter rivalry twixt Percy and Douglas is nowhere better understood than at Otterburn, where Percy's Cross stands a few hundred yards north of the A696 heading out beyond the village. The battle, to be re-enacted by the Redesdale Society in 1988 is one of the best retold in border balladry, and a permanent exhibition is to be set up nearby.

Further north, efforts are being made to improve the site of Flodden, certainly the largest and, in terms of casualties, the bloodiest battle fought on Northumbrian soil. Though the essential landscape remains, drainage and cultivation have robbed the site of an appropriate sombre air. Pastoral calm belies the intensity of the slaughter where a Renaissance prince and his court perished in a bloody Gotterdammerung more befitting a Dark Age chieftain and his housecarls.

The border itself, largely unchanged and unchanging; the Raid of the Reidswire is now witnessed by a plaque and the walk from the car park at Carter Bar repays the effort. Nowhere, perhaps, is the harsh environment of the border more visible, or the uncompromising toughness of its past inhabitants more easily understood. One of history's earliest and most beleaguered frontiers, a season of strife which stretched for a millenium and a half and, like Macbeth, 'Steep'd in Blood'.

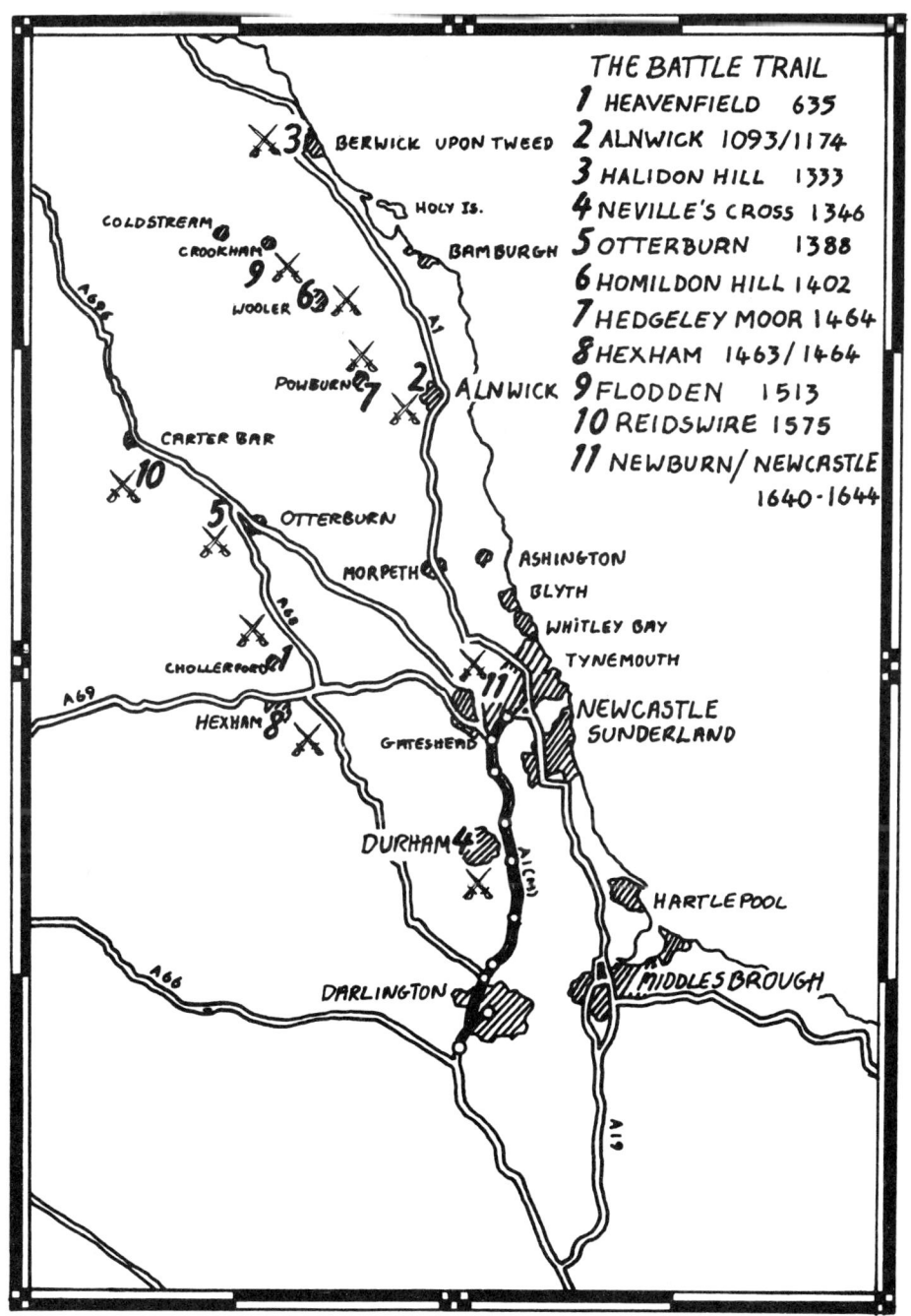

THE BATTLE TRAIL
1 HEAVENFIELD 635
2 ALNWICK 1093/1174
3 HALIDON HILL 1333
4 NEVILLE'S CROSS 1346
5 OTTERBURN 1388
6 HOMILDON HILL 1402
7 HEDGELEY MOOR 1464
8 HEXHAM 1463/1464
9 FLODDEN 1513
10 REIDSWIRE 1575
11 NEWBURN/ NEWCASTLE
1640-1644

Introduction

Northumberland is a county of battlefields — from Romans to Roundheads, armies have marched and countermarched over its many acres. In the centuries before the Union many a Scottish king used the eastern seaboard as his key into England, and more than one had cause to regret, most were glad to see the Tweed again and there was an abundance of those who left their bones to bleach on Northumbrian soil. Malcolm, victor of Shakespeare's Macbeth, fell to a Northumbrian lance before the walls of Alnwick and James, that proud renaissance prince, was hacked to a ghastly death at Flodden.

The battlefield was not the sole prerogative of princes; great lords and commoners too could settle their feuds in blood. Northumbrian history would never be the same without the celebrated enmity of Douglas and Percy which produced some considerable slaughter, the very stuff of balladry. A good few notches further down the social scale were the raiders and reivers who kept the wild border aflame for centuries, a unique blend of farmer cum rustler cum guerilla whose feuds, skirmishes and forays could fill several volumes on their own.

It is often difficult to draw a line between a battle: 'Combat, especially between large organised forces' and a skirmish: 'A piece of irregular, or unpremeditated fighting' — the difference to anyone inolved is likely to be academic at best. Dark Age and medieval armies often tended to lack cohesion or regular formation and most invasions were simply large scale forays aimed more at widespread looting than any significant military objective. The reiver may have lacked the style or chivalry of his betters but his motivation was usually the same.

The warrings of the past appear clumsy and often insignificant compared to more refined horrors of modern warfare which can spread death and devastation on a scale undreamt of in earlier times. Then, however, there was none of the vicarious violence of high altitude bombing, massive artillery bombardment or automatic weapons. Broadsword and mace seem practically benign compared with napalm and phosphorous grenades. Then, warfare was contained, the fate of the nations decided upon a piece of ground hardly bigger than a football pitch. Combat itself was generally hand to hand and though the horrors of such encounters pale beside more civilised means, it was terrible enough. The nightmare then was the hissing hail of yard long arrows, the sickening shock of impact as bodies of mounted knights crashed in bloody mêlée. Limbs severed, bodies mangled, bloody entrails spreading beneath the strokes of crude but deadly weaponry, wielded with all the strength of desperation and the skill of long association.

We might ask why it is necessary to relive the horrors of the past, when the present has horrors enough of its own — more than enough in fact. Few of history's wildest villains ever dreamt of genocide or nuclear holocaust. This could be merely because they lacked the means rather than the motivation . It is an inescapable fact that much of Northumberland's earlier history revolves around the battlefield and the men who steered the course of her history were wont to solve their problems with steel rather than words. Furthermore we are fortunate that as several of these battles were decided away from the spread of urbanisation many sites remain substantially unaltered — Northumberland could yet provide a ripe market for the current vogue for 'battlefield tours' where we armchair generals can enjoy the exploits of our ancestors without any of the attendant perils. It is often only too easy, with the inevitable benefit of hindsight, to criticise the actions of past commanders but few of us who do have had to take any of the same decisions in similar circumstances. Rationality can often disappear beneath an empty belly and fear is a more likely master than reason when the arrows fly and the axes swing.

In any event the men of Heavenfield and Flodden needed few lessons in courage or ferocity and it was these qualities that formed the pattern of Northumbrian life for many centuries and hopefully have not been entirely lost even today.

A revival of interest in historical conflict in recent years has led to the staging of 'battle re-enactments'. These can be seen as detailed experiments in history or pure escapism depending, largely, upon your point of view — the truth probably lies somewhere between the two.

Re-enactment really started with the 'Sealed Knot', a society who re-fight the battles of the English Civil War. Membership now runs to several thousands and musters can be quite spectacular. A great deal of emphasis is placed upon historical accuracy in matters of dress, discipline, weapons and accoutrement. The original society now has competition from numerous others.

In addition to the English Civil War societies other groups concentrate upon Saxon and Viking, Medieval, Napoleonic, American Civil War and Second World War re-enactments, ranging from small local groups to national organisations. Some, particularly the Napoleonic and WWII societies go to considerable lengths to ensure that members have the correct gear and understand the drill and tactics of the era in question.

Some groups have been branded as 'militarist' but this is pure nonsense, for most re-enactment is simply an interesting hobby that offers the vicarious thrill of combat with none, or virtually none, of the attendant risks.

More ambitious than any form of re-enactment, war-gaming etc. the Soviet Union has seen an attempt to permanently re-create one particular battlefield. Operations began recently to restore the ground at Borodino to the conditions prevailing at the time of the epic, hugely bloody encounter of 1812. The 'restoration' involves the rebuilding of such key strongpoints as the Raevsky Redoubt, the Bagration Fleches etc. in addition to considerable amounts of clearance and landscaping. Quite an undertaking — equal to the Corporation of Newcastle deciding to restore the site of the battle of Newburn, reconstructing the ill-fated redoubts, altering the flow of the Tyne back to its course in 1640, and demolishing such later additions as Stella Power Station and Newburn Bridge!

It seems unlikely either that without a markedly more buoyant economy or a state sponsored programme that any northern battlefield will ever benefit from the 'Borodino' treatment, though most British battlefields are marked, few are venerated or exploited. Why indeed should we commemorate a site where hundreds or even thousands fell in usually pointless butchery, probably without ever knowing exactly where they were or why? On the other hand a battlefield is, in its own way, as much of an ancient monument as other far more tangible remains. Most were typical of their time, some passed without notice, but others had major social or political consequences. The fight at Hexham, 1464, marked a definite end in a phase of the Wars of the Roses, the carnage at Flodden removed the flower of Scottish nobility for a whole generation, and Heavenfield was a great triumph for the Church of Christ over the Heathen host.

The sites of some particularly celebrated encounters have benefited from the impetus of tourism, perhaps most noticeably in Scotland where the National Trust has assumed responsibility for Culloden and Killiecrankie. The former field has been amply endowed with a thick veneer of the romanticism that has been applied to the Jacobite movement in general though it is difficult to imagine than any of the ill-fated clansmen charging uphill to their deaths on Drummossie Moor would ever understand how. Nevertheless thousands now pay to enter the museum and visitor centre, to see the pathetic cluster of clan graves and the aptly named 'Well of the Dead', there is even a film show.

In many ways Northumbria has much to offer this revival of interest in ancient combat, many were the Viking raids that did occur along the coast in the years prior to the Norman conquest, and although we can never overlook the appalling savagery and utter brutality that followed in the wake of marching armies their campaigns are a very real part of our history. If such a thing as the 'National Character' exists then it was moulded in the blood and fire of these ages. Predatory Norsemen, marauding Scots, mailed seigneurs, vainglorious knights, freebooting mosstroopers, and dour covenanters all set the pattern of their own age and helped lay the foundations of our own.

Chapter One

CELT, SAXON AND DANE

Northumberland is one of England's largest and most northerly counties, enclosing an area of some two thousand square miles. The scenery comprises some of the loveliest and most varied, from the pleasant sandy beaches and rocky headlands, to lush green dales and valleys, rolling, tussocky hills and high untamed moorland of peat bog and heather.

The highest point, at 2,676 feet above sea level, is the Cheviot massif itself, the surviving stump of an ancient volcano, ground down by the millennia into the backbone of a range of rounded hills towering squat and massive along the border line.

Further south lie the ranges of Fell sandstone, none more striking than Simonside where cold rock and barren heather tower over the fertile valley below. Southward again from the sandstone hills lies more moorland which fades into the lowland plain that sweeps around the heights within. A last but remarkable feature is the great Whin Sill, that springs forth in fine dramatic form to carry the ramparts of Hadrian's Wall upon its western march.

Northumberland was one of the last counties to receive its final boundaries in the mid-nineteenth century and was again altered by the restructuring of local government in 1974. By then, however, man had been here for at least five millennia and boundary changes could easily be made by a stroke of the bureaucrat's pen, rather than by a stroke of the axe or broadsword as in the past.

It appears that the earliest inhabitants arrived during the period of the Middle Stone Age, sometime between 5,000-3,000 B.C. These may have been related to a larger group already established in Durham and North Yorkshire. Around 2,500 B.C. the New Stone Age had begun and some finds from this period have emerged. In the era immediately before the Bronze Age a fresh wave of immigrants arrived, this group has been labelled by archaeologists as the 'Beaker' people, so called from the distinctive shaping of their pottery. Again, it is possible that these people were a branch of a colony from further south or they may have come directly from the continent. In either event the colonisation was essentially an amphibious operation. The lowland areas of the county were still densely forested and almost impenetrable to these

17

early settlers, therefore they came by boat using the rivers as highways and establishing their colonies along the accessible valleys of the Rede and the Coquet.

The advent of the Bronze Age saw a sudden swelling of the previously diminutive population which in turn led to a spread of colonisation into hitherto uninhabited areas such as South Tynedale.

The initial rush of Iron Age colonists into southern Britain around 500 B.C. did not have a similar, immediate impact in the north, which remained very much of a cultural backwater, and, into which the Iron Age came more as a trickle than a torrent. Caesar's early expeditions can hardly have affected the Northumbrians at all, and even the great invasion of 43 A.D. had no instant effect. It was not until Agricola's advance of 79-80 A.D., following the conquest of the Brigantes, that the iron shod tramp of legions was heard in the north.

Agricola had pushed the frontier northward some forty years before Hadrian ordered the building of the great wall, that was to leave such an indelible print upon the Northumbrian landscape. Nonetheless, Agricola was still quick to spot the significance of the Tyne-Solway gap. He established a network of roads, supply depots and garrisons along the line of his great east-west highway, the Stanegate. Corbridge was developed at the vital junction with Dere Street on its northward course through Redesdale, where it too was looked after by a chain of camps, including the remote post at Chew Green, whose forbidding location could hardly have made it one of the more popular imperial postings.

A third road, The Devils Causeway, probed eastward to the coast, passing through Ryal, Hartburn and Bridge of Aln. The wall, begun after Hadrian's visit in 120 A.D. and completed in the years 122-128, is undoubtedly the most impressive Roman undertaking in Britain. Beneath its sheltering ramparts the Pax Romana was to flourish for nearly three hundred years.

It seems that it was the Pax Romana which promoted the development of many Iron Age settlements and that many of the counties' hill forts belong to the Romano-British, rather than the pre Roman, era. Though a few were already here, it does appear that the growth of the majority was fostered by the security of Roman rule. The overall useful life of many a hilltop site was preserved, by dint of its defensive potential, even long after the Eagles had departed and the free for all of the Dark Ages had begun. Some writers have even gone so far as to suggest that they remained in use, at least as temporary refuges, until well into the Middle Ages.

The history of the wall itself was not without, quite literally, its ups and downs. Internal strife within the empire, sporadic moves to reoccupy the abandoned Agricolan provinces to the north, and the Antonine wall, meant that there were several long intervals of decay and neglect. It was overrun when the garrison was withdrawn in 296, and again in 367. After this latter collapse the frontier was restored by Theodosius, but the defence of the wall from then on became entrusted more and more to local levies and foederatii of friendly tribes, such as the Votadini. Thus, even after the final withdrawal of 410, the wall was not entirely defenceless and abandoned, though for how long the Celts could cling to this bulwark of their inheritance was debatable in the extreme.

Without the military and administrative might of Rome behind it the wall became little more than a rather fatuous heap of stone, still impressive but basically untenable. Never intended as a defence against a major invasion, but more as a base for forward operations from which an enemy could be outflanked and then pinned down, the wall soon became redundant; there was none capable of maintaining its potential.

Legend does make some mention of the wall in this uncertain period and one story places the location of Arthur's last and fatal encounter with the traitor Mordred, the battle of Camlann, at Birdoswald on the wall. Such theories are more than enticing but, sadly, lack foundation and must remain forever in that twilight era where history and myth overlap and entwine.

Nearer to reality, and sometime around the year 547, the Angle leader Ida and his followers sailed northward from their base in Yorkshire, hugging the coast all the way, much as the prehistoric settlers had done. Tradition has always cited Bamburgh as their eventual landfall. This beachhead was to form the nucleus of the new kingdom of Bernicia. The first settlement was named Dinguardi, and others followed at Berneich (Berwick) and Guarth (Warkworth). This thin coastal strip remained the limit of the Saxons' foothold for several decades. Effective expansion was blocked by the still virile Celtic kingdom of Reged, which seems to have covered central Northumberland, parts of Cumberland and the Scottish borderland. Under its warrior king Urien the newcomers were contained.

From his capital at Errleon (location unknown), Urien twice defeated the sons of Ida, once at the passage of the Waren Ford and again, resoundingly, in Upper Coquetdale. After the prince was slain however, Reged swiftly crumbled and the Saxons surged forward in an orgy of expansion, until all we now call Northumberland was theirs at last.

New enemies now came forward. Chief amongst these early foes was Aedan, the Celtic king of Dalriada, who swept through Bernicia driving Ethelfrid, the king, and his followers southward. Cautious after these early reverses, Ethelfrid chose with care his moment to pounce upon the victorious Celts, smashing them utterly at the battle of Daegsanstan (Dissington), and scattering them back beyond the bounds of his infant kingdom.

The victory gave Ethelfrid a taste for conquest. Secure in the north he was able to turn greedy eyes southward to where, stretching from the Tees to the Humber, lay the Anglian kingdom of Deira.

A youth named Edwin was heir to the throne but soon found himself an outlaw, when Ethelfrid swept through his kingdom and added it to his domains by right of conquest. From now on Ethelfrid's path was marked by fire and sword, so much so that he earned the unenviable epithet of 'Fleasaurus', or 'Destroyer'. For the next decade he raided far and wide, scourging the lands beyond the frontiers of his new principality.

His generalship was sufficient to wrest the old Roman fortress of Chester from its Celtic defenders. At last, inevitably, his luck ran out and Ethelfrid fell, sword in hand, fighting his fellow Saxons who had chosen to support the disinherited prince of Deira, Edwin, upon whose shoulders rested the joint mantle of Deira and Bernicia. It was now the year 617.

Edwin was wed to a princess of the Kentish royal family, long since converts to Christ, and it was undoubtedly her influence which secured the monk Paulinus' visit to the north. The campaign for Jesus was a resounding success, the king was himself baptised in 627, releasing a flood of converts who flocked to the cross in droves. At Holystone, on the Coquet, Paulinus is said to have baptised no less than three thousand souls.

From his palace at Gefrin[1], Edwin administered a kingdom that stretched from the Humber to the Forth, and from Lindisfarne to the Solway. Ida's coastal strip had become the mighty kingdom of Northumbria. Edwin's rule came to an untimely close beneath the blade of Penda, that redoubtable heathen and king of Mercia, who slew the Northumbrian king in battle at Hatfield, on the Severn.

Now it was a son of the formidable Ethelfrid who succeeded. Named Enfrid, the new monarch reigned just long enough to fall against the ravaging hordes of the Celtic Welshman Cadwallon who sacked Northumbria from coast to coast. The emergence of the new kingdom and the chrysalis of Christianity in the north seemed equally precarious, until a momentous victory at Heavenfield, won by Enfrid's brother Oswald, saved the kingdom and the cross.

Even Oswald however was not proof against the might of the savage

[1] Now known as Yeavering.

Penda, and he too went the way of his predecessors, too soon and too bloody. It was a third son of Ethelfrid, Oswi, destined for a brilliant reign of nearly three decades, who finally put paid to this heathen scourge. Oswi had spent some time on Iona and was accompanied upon his return to Northumbria by a number of monks from that place. These particular clerics, with their Celtic version of the gospels, clashed with the more generally acceptable Roman version. Nevertheless, it was the Celtic monks who ushered in the great period of Northumbrian monasticism, even though the doctrinal differences were eventually settled in favour of Rome.

Throughout the eighth century A.D. Northumbrian culture and learning flourished, this age was truly the Golden Age and it was not until the end of the century that a cloud, or rather a sail, appeared on the horizon. It was in fact in 793 that the Holy Island of Lindisfarne added to its distinction by suffering the unenviable privilege of sustaining the first attack of the sea-raiders. It was here that people first learned to dread the sight of the great striped sails and dragon's head prows of the Norsemen, and here that the first fury of their onslaught was felt.

It was a grim omen. Before the next century was a decade old Northumbria reeled before the Viking scourge. The learning of centuries was swept away and almost obliterated by a torrent of death and destruction. The centres of religion and culture were a favourite target for the Norse heathens, who pillaged and slew almost at will, brushing aside the few attempts at armed resistance in a welter of blood.

Though few ever came to settle, the increasing severity of the raids hastened the decline of the kingdom of Northumbria, which, in a surprisingly short time, plummeted from its earlier zenith to a miserable nadir. Soon the far flung boundaries began to crumble, borders that had cost so much blood to define were soon under new attack.

Strathclyde, the kingdom of the west, soon ate up the lands around the Solway. More Norsemen, from entrenched settlements in the midlands, prised free Lancashire and Cumbria. In the north the pressing might of the emergent Scots nation swept through the Lothians to the banks of the Tweed.

Northumbria was sinking fast in the face of these combined inroads, benumbed beneath the Viking fury. The tide that was to turn back the Norsemen rose in Wessex and soon engulfed the crippled northern kingdom in its fresh exuberance. By 927 the men from the south were in firm control of the north. The decline of Northumbria was now complete; wasted and reduced by ceaseless harrying the emaciated kingdom was shrunk into a mere Earldom, a status that was maintained until the Norman conquest. Though free at last of the Viking menace, the Scots, as predators, proved worthy successors, and the earldom like the kingdom before suffered much from invaders.

Throughout the Dark Ages, and indeed for long after, warfare was a constant fact of life, in spite of which few commanders of the period had anything approaching the well drilled military machine that their predecessors the Romans, possessed. Indeed, the warriors of the Dark Age would have been dismissed as gangs of disorganised barbarians by the men of the Legions.

War was essentially a tribal or clan event, the rudimentary agrarian economy could not provide large forces for lengthy campaigns. Armies would always seek a swift decisive victory, followed by a pleasant interlude given over to the pleasures of pillage and rapine. Then, honour, greed and lust appeased, they would load up the loot and head for home, there to lick their wounds and prepare for winter. Once the snows had closed in, the deeds of battle would be transformed by the bards into the work of heroes.

Battles were often wont to be haphazard and disorganised, often little better than a giant mêlée, decided on a hand to hand basis with forces locked in bloody embrace, skill, strength and fortune to decide the day. Individual kings and chieftains would gird themselves with an iron ring of semi-professional armed retainers, House Carls, who would provide a steel tipped backbone for any host or levy.

The bulk of forces were levied from the populace on a strictly part time basis, and thus the host or Fyrd went as often to war as they went to the fields, with a minimum of specialised military hardware. Expensive items of accoutrement such as the mail shirt, or Byrnie, were more usually reserved for the warlord and his retainers. Lesser mortals would either go unarmoured, or rely on homemade protection, plain leather jerkins, bare or reinforced with sewn plates of bone or metal.

The most basic form of headgear was the simple iron, or leather banded with iron, skull. More sophisticated and therefore more rare and costly items were few though a chieftain might boast a helmet of the 'Sutton Hoo' type with sculptured face piece. Shields were light and rounded, a timber frame covered with layers of hide and surmounted by a metal boss.

The long-handled battleaxe was a favourite weapon in an army where the footsoldier predominated; handled with skill and strength it could produce fearful slaughter in a mêlée, especially against an unarmoured foe. A lighter, shorter shafted axe was reserved for throwing, whilst true close quarter combat might be settled by the long bladed dirk or 'scramasaxe'. Swords themselves, a double edged yard long blade surmounted by straight quillons with a simple shaft and pommel, were a weapon to be prized. Those unable to afford such true children of the battlefield were forced to rely on simple spears or modified agricultural implements — crude and basic, but it was the plain English bill hook that levelled the Scottish host at Flodden, and a screaming horde of like-armed highlanders routed two redcoat armies as late as 1745.

Battle Shield Haugh, 572-592, NT882102

Rome's North-west Frontier — Hadrian's Wall astride the Whin Sill.

The story of this affray is born out of the mouths of generations of illiterate bards, who made up for their academic deficiencies with a plentiful supply of poetic licence and a diplomatic deference to whoever that night's host may have been. Therefore history is shrouded in myth and romance, clouded with the repetition of ages, with few opportunities for fanciful embroidery being overlooked. Bearing this in mind, it does seem feasible to suggest that an encounter of the nature described did take place in the far reaches of Upper Coquetdale at some time in the period noted.

We know that Urien, the Celtic prince of Reged, fought vigorously against the encroaching power of the Anglian newcomers who probed and feinted at his kingdom from the safety of their established coastal bases. Though once defeated at the Waren Ford, the leader of the Saxon host, Flamdwyn, son of Ida, gathered his forces for a determined thrust at Erlleon, the chief hold of Reged.

Flamdwyn is known as the 'Flame-bearer' an epithet that speaks more for his enthusiasm than his ability. Advancing his host in four divisions he pushed along the banks of the Coquet marching almost unopposed into the hilly country surrounding the heart of the Celtic kingdom. The strength of the Saxon force is unknown, though nothing short of a full scale army could penetrate so far, or so boldly, into enemy territory.

Once Alwinton was reached however, the swift and certain nature of the advance seems to have fallen prey to some uncertainty. The march along the Coquet had been an easy passage by a clear route, plenty of open country and little fear of surprise, the host easy to marshall and deploy. Beyond Alwinton things were very different. Without considerable local knowledge, or detailed reconnaissance, a continued advance was fraught with difficulty and with peril. The broken hilly country offered little sight of a definite objective and the tangle of steep sided glens offered hiding for a dozen armies. The choices before the 'Flame-bearer' were simple — he could advance into uncertainty, or retreat into ignominy. He chose the former.

It was to be a costly mistake. His scouts had informed him that a Celtic host was gathering some three or four miles away in the valley of the Usway Burn. Doomed by his own impetuosity, the Saxon chief hurled his lumbering host along the narrow valley floor. It can hardly have been a happy march, the Saxons were, by now, a long way from home and the swift conquest they had hoped for had not materialised. Instead, they stumbled into a remote and forbidding glen, hustled by blank unfamiliar hills, advancing to meet a foe of uncertain strength, set to fight for the ground where he was born.

They were not to be kept long in anticipation. High above the valley floor the Celts, led by Urien their king, were already drawn up in battle order. Whether this was on Shillhope Law, or along the ridge from Copper Snout, to Saughty Hill is uncertain, but their position was undoubtedly commanding. It must certainly have seemed so to the Saxons when they finally hove into view, for the advance ground to a dead halt. Apparently undismayed by the powerful array, Flamdwyn boldly tried to bluster his way clear of trouble, by arrogantly demanding hostages from the Celts.

The bluff however, was not successful, and with a mighty chorus of anger and derision, the Celtic host swept down upon their foes clustered far below, venting their formidable rage in an onslaught of terrific fury. Suddenly, the proud Saxon host were truly on the defensive, as the weight of the charge burst upon them like a steel crested tidal wave, smashing through their already demoralised ranks.

It was altogether too much for the invaders, panic, and then a rout, ensued. Down the length of the Usway Burn and along the wide and verdant valley of the Coquet the Saxons fled, harried all the way by the victorious Celts. The retreat must have indeed been a nightmare, with slaughter enough to satisfy the bards for ages, a host of Saxons slain upon the field itself and doubtless many more hacked to bloody death in the narcotic frenzy of the pursuit.

That day upon the banks of the Usway Burn was a great day for the Celts and a truly great day for Urien, their prince. The boundaries of the kingdom had been secured and the encroaching enemy given a bloody nose to boot. It would be some time before the Saxons felt bold or confident enough to venture far from their coastal holds, though even there they were not safe, as the Celts now swept down from their upland fastnesses to wreak havoc of their own amongst the invaders.

This was a truly low ebb of Anglian vitality, as they were forced to abandon dreams of conquest merely to hold on to their present meagre gains. The triumph was to be shortlived, history can be postponed but not avoided. Urien fell by the dagger of some petty, jealous assassin, who undoubtedly hastened his own demise by causing that of his chief. Their champion slain, the Celts withdrew first to the hills, and then into legend and the Saxons came once more, and this time without real opposition, leaving the shattered kingdom of Reged as food only for the mournful bards.

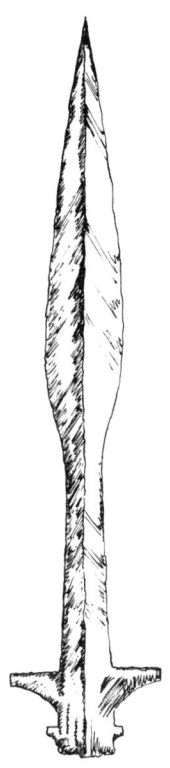

'Winged' Spear-head 8th-11th Century.

Ironically, the far reaches of Upper Coquetdale still reverberate to the din of war, though now it is less in earnest, and most of the warriors depart after the weekend is over. Despite the proximity of the Artillery Ranges, a walk along the valley of the Usway Burn by the track from Shillmoor discloses a landscape little altered from that which rose to greet the Saxon host. As we tread the same route as those distant warriors the same waters ripple gently by and the same hills crowd the horizons, equally as remote, and just as stunningly lovely as in the lost days of Reged.

Heavenfield, 635, NY936695.

The task of defending Northumbria from Cadwallon and his rapacious hordes was scarcely enviable, the kingdom had barely had time to recover from the last incursion, and Oswald, hastily marshalling those forces he could muster, could not hope to match the invaders' numbers.

The Welsh seem to have marched northward from York along the line of Dere Street, the old Roman highway doubtless still providing a line of march, even though any who were capable of maintaining its surface had departed with the Eagles. Their advance would take the invaders through Corbridge, and Oswald hoping to intercept them thereafter, took up a defensive position some four miles north of Hexham.

The site of this position is now known as Heavenfield, where the army facing to the east had its northern flank protected by a rocky escarpment, presumably Brady's Crag, and its southern flank covered by the line of the Wall itself, still, a formidable obstacle, even two centuries after its abandonment.

Meanwhile the Welsh, in the full panoply of war, were approaching, a streaming horde of Celtic warriors, swinging left from Stagshaw and pushing westward along the northern side of the Wall, full of the courage born of numbers, and the memory of easy victory.

Bede, who was writing at a time when details of the fight were clearly remembered, and not yet embroidered by bardic fancies, tells us that Oswald was accompanied by Cuthbert and a monkish contingent who had erected a wooden cross that served the army as a standard, for the church, as much as the state, had cause to fear the heathen's wrath. As the Welsh vanguard appeared upon the skyline, the king, kneeling before the cross, led his men in prayer — the sight of so large an enemy host must have convinced even the most lukewarm Christians in the ranks of the pressing need for divine intervention:

'Let us all bow the knee and together pray the almighty God living and true that he will, in his mercy save us from the proud and savage enemy, as he knows that we have undertaken a just war for the salvation of our nation.'

The resounding chorus of 'Amen' that no doubt followed would have gladdened the heart of any cleric in different circumstances, but now that prayers were over the serious business of killing could begin in earnest.

And it was indeed in deadly earnest as the first shock of impact resounded upon the Northumbrian line. In the hacking, stabbing, slashing frenzy that followed neither side could make any headway against the other. Hemmed in by the narrow front, the Welsh were unable to deploy their superior numbers to outflank and swamp the

Anglo Saxon
King of the early
7th Century — he
wears a helmet
with sculpted face
mask of the
'Sutton Hoo'
type, mail and
splented greaves.

Northumbrians whose stout and determined defence was robbing the invaders of the easy triumph they had so carelessly anticipated.

We do not know how long the fight lasted or how many men fell beneath the long axes of their opponents. Even the deeds of valour of which the bards would sing, so that a man's children, or grandchildren, might know he had fought that day for their birthright, are now forgotten. Who it was that first began the trickle that became the flood of panic is also lost, but soon the Welsh had had enough — they had come for wine and plunder not to see their life blood spewed out upon some foreign soil.

As they broke, the Northumbrian line swept forward like a torrent bursting with the anger and hate of past humiliations. Hemmed by the Wall the Welsh scrabbled vainly for some toehold to aid their southward flight, but the avenging blades of Oswald's men were everywhere, turning the rout into a massacre. Beneath the cold grey crags of Fallowfield Fell the Welshmen were cut down like rabbits. It was at Moulds Close, aptly named perhaps, that the greatest slaughter took place, though the fleeing Celts were harried across the breadth of Acomb Fell and even down the length of the Devilswater. Here, legend relates, that redoubtable heathen, Cadwallon himself, was finally brought to ground and slain, along with countless of his countrymen, whose stripped and stiffened corpses marked the flight in a twisting blaze of carnage.

The battle of Heavenfield proved utterly decisive. Oswald had, from a desperate holding action, wrested a brilliant victory, scattering his enemies to the wind and laying their chief and many others beside in their graves. How many the Welsh lost is not known though the slaughter must have been terrific. Both the church and kingdom were saved, and though the latter would eventually decline, the flame of Christianity that had fluttered in the strong heathen wind would never be so threatened again. In the struggle between Christian and pagan, Heavenfield was a milestone, however undesirable it should be that the word of God be passed on by a bloodbath.

At present the site of the battle is amply commemorated, not only by the cross at the side of the road, but also by the Church of St. Oswald. The bulk of the present building dates from 1737 and was 'Gothicized' by W. Hicks in 1887. An earlier chapel may well have stood upon the site, indeed a silver coin of Oswald with his head upon one side and the cross upon the reverse, is said to have been uncovered during the reign of Elizabeth I.

Actual details of the numbers of men involved are scanty, to say the least, and even the best of estimates is little more than inspired and careful guesswork. We can perhaps surmise that the Northumbrian force being scratchbuilt, and in some desperation, was not more than a few thousand strong, the Welsh perhaps three or four times as strong. Losses again are a matter of guesswork, some Northumbrians undoubtedly fell, though those injured could at least expect succour. Not so for the Welsh, apart from the slaughter of the rout, few wounded or stragglers could expect much in the way of clemency from the victors, the Northumbrians being too much hardened by their earlier sufferings.

The battle shows Oswald had a good grasp of tactics, his choice for the site was ideal for an army so outnumbered by their foes, with both flanks well covered and the rear protected by the sharp drop down to Chollerford. The Welsh, on the hand, contributed considerably to their own downfall by rushing so rashly to the attack without obviously considering the nature of the ground.

Even after this momentous victory, Northumbria was not yet free of the pagan horde, for that redoubtable rogue Penda, King of Mercia, was still very much alive and still able to account for Oswald who fell beneath his blade at Maserfield, in Shropshire, after only eight short but fruitful years upon the throne of the kingdom he had saved.

The site lies adjacent to the Military Road, the B6318, and, as mentioned, is marked by the roadside memorial. The battlefield itself is crowned by the church whose location offers an excellent vantage.

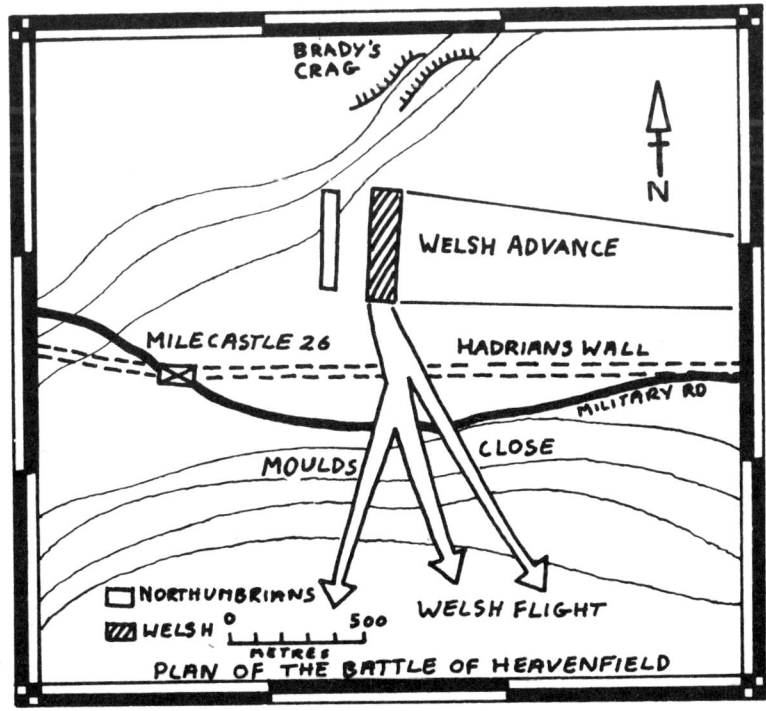

PLAN OF THE BATTLE OF HEAVENFIELD

Carham, 838, NT798381.

The era of the Norse raids produced many often bloody encounters and skirmishes, some of which have undoubtedly been forgotten. In many cases it was sheer desperation that prompted the hard pressed inhabitants to resist as the inroads bit deeper and deeper into the troubled kingdom.

As time went by the coastal areas would have become so despoiled as to provide little return for an expedition, consequently the inland areas, previously spared, began to suffer also. Furthermore, as the raids probed deeper, the earlier refuge of a swift flight inland would no longer suffice.

In the engagements that did take place the pattern of the fight seems to have been dismally predictable. Ill prepared and equipped levies, dragged literally from the fields in an attempt to stem the savage tide of Norsemen invariably succumbed to the barbaric elan of the raiders. Apart from their superior morale and natural propensity for mayhem, the Vikings were also generally far better armed and armoured than their indigenous opponents.

The fight at Carham was to be no exception to this bloody norm. The village itself lies on the northern rim of the present county of Northumberland, but in the ninth century the Tweed was not then recognised as the border line, and the kingdom of Northumbria still held lands in the Lothians.

Of the battle itself we know relatively little. It is generally accepted that a force of Vikings that had made landfall on or near Lindisfarne, was proceeding by degrees along the valley of the Tweed pillaging at will until, at Carham, they were opposed by an English force. In the mêlée that ensued the Saxons were decimated, with a considerable number of the poorly armed levies being cut down by the long blades of the Norsemen, who also accounted for no less than two counts and eleven bishops!

It appears from the number of English notables slain that the force must have been quite sizeable, presumably hoping that numbers alone might offer some proof against the weapons and esprit de corps of the raiders. In this they were obviously totally mistaken and once the size of the force had failed to overawe the attackers the demonic fury of the Norse charge soon decided the issue.

In all fairness the Vikings must indeed have been formidable opponents, worthy of respect from even the most seasoned campaigner, and easily enough to turn raw levies to quivering panic. We can only imagine the Viking force as it must have appeared streaking across the ground toward the wavering ranks; the sun glinting from shirts of mail and burnished helms, tough, heavily muscled warriors hardened by days at the oars and the fury of the seasons, swords and axes swung in deadly earnest.

We cannot now identify the exact spot at which the conflict occurred, though legend asserts that a field just south of the village itself marks the location. Interestingly enough, the adjoining field is known as 'Wallaces Croft' where, again largely according to legend, the Scottish hero is said to have encamped one night in 1296, whilst engaged on a foray against England. Doubtless he, at least, did not have the inclination to ruminate on past encounters, as he was more than occupied with those of the present.

The fertile valley of the Tweed was far from free of the tramp of marching feet and the din of battle. Countless forays were yet to be made and fought across it and even Carham was to lend its name to another fight, though this took place in 1018, and was actually fought nearer Wark — more of that later.

Battle Bridge, 875, NU119122.

This slightly later attempt to ward off a Viking inroad followed almost the same sanguinary pattern as the former attempt at Carham, some forty years before.

The English were of a different generation but still far from ready to tackle the fury of the Norsemen who, themselves, had certainly not mellowed with time.

On this occasion the raiders appeared to have landed at Alnmouth and followed their familiar course of devastation along the banks of the river until their crossing of the Edlingham Burn was opposed.

By this the Saxons presumably hoped to save Whittingham Vale from the raiders attentions. Their position, flanked by the Aln on the left, prevented any outflanking movements and therefore gave them some advantage.

This came to naught however, when the Norsemen made a direct attack on the ford itself, presumably using their superior arms and armour to force a passage. The crossing was not gained without a sharp struggle, indeed the Edlingham Burn is said to have run red for three days and nights thereafter. Most of the blood, inevitably, being that from the indigenous inhabitants, who fell by the score, the rest being scattered once the Norsemen consolidated their hold upon the ford.

In the end the battle proved yet another salutory lesson for the hard-pressed Northumbrians — those who survived to benefit by the experience but did nothing to halt the regularity and destructiveness of the raids.

The Vikings.

The site of the battle is not marked, though the hamlet of Battlebridge commemorates the encounter. There is little of immediate interest to recommend to the visitor.

Wandon, 937?, NU040281.

Wandon hardly ranks amongst the most famous of Northumberland's battlefields, perhaps because it has always been overshadowed by the battle of Brunanburh with which it has also often been confused. Though no precise location for the latter engagement has ever been forthcoming, the facts of the battle and the combatants themselves were very similar.

Athelstan, a warrior king of England, who had waged an unending but repeatedly successful war against the Norsemen and for whom the tide had at last begun to turn, had also extended his dominion to cover most of Northumbria. More of the ailing kingdom's lands came under his control when, in 925, he at last got hold of Bamburgh, even then a key coastal fortress.

His new northern province was entrusted to two Earls, Alfgar and Godric, the latter of whom was swiftly slain in battle against the Norse chief Anlaf the Red. This success encouraged the defection of two of Athelstan's Cumbrian Earls, Adils and Hrings, who brought their forces to join Anlaf at his encampment near Vinheide (Wandon) two miles east of Wooler and two miles north west of Chillingham.

The defeated Alfgar, who had escaped the slaughter in which his co-ruler fell had alerted Athelstan to the Danish peril and the king, not one to brook the slaying of one of his minions, swiftly assembled his army and came by stages to confront the host encamped at Wandon.

A formal challenge was given and accepted and the commanders agreed that their forces should fight upon the plain between Hepburn Wood and the banks of the Till. It was at the narrow neck of this alluvial tract that the English made their camp, perhaps near Bewick?

Once this almost Homeric scene had been set, Alfgar, perhaps to atone for the disgrace of surviving when his comrade died, was given the task of commanding the vanguard and probing the enemy's strength. This first advance was met by a counter thrust led by the renegade Cumbrian earls who severely discomforted the Northumbrians with their vastly superior numbers. Consequently, the van retired somewhat more swiftly than they had advanced, and in some disorder, leaving Alfgar with the unenviable task of explaining yet another debacle to his choleric monarch. True to his colours the Earl took the course of least resistance and fled, doubtless one dose of the royal wrath was more than enough.

Athelstan was not given time, perhaps fortunately for Alfgar, to ruminate upon his lordlings desertion for the Cumbrians, bolstered by their early success, were still advancing. To stem this oncoming tide the king sent forth a mixed division of English and Norse allies led by a brace of fighting brothers, named Egil and Thorolf. In the clash that followed as English, Norse and Northumbrian fought against more Norse and Cumbrian foes, the former were victorious. Of the rebel earls Hrings was slain and Adils driven into the woods, where, safe from immediate pursuit, he attempted to rally the survivors of his scattered band.

This initial skirmishing, reminiscent of the heroic duelling of forgotten Dark Age chieftains, brought the first day of the battle to a close. In the gathering darkness scavengers would scour the field for loot whilst the armies waited for the morrow, when the serious business of slaughter could begin.

In the dim, uncertain light of the early dawn the two hosts moved up to contest the plain in earnest, the pale sunlight splashing across a sea of glinting mail, crested by a razor honed wave of silent spears, serried in

33

awful anticipation. Athelstan commanded the English left, that wing nearest the river, whilst trusty Thorolf took the right marching parallel to the woods.

Suddenly the foe loomed into view, the pace quickened, hearts began to beat faster, and fear, every man's spur, jogged the combatants forward toward their fate. War was suddenly no longer a fanciful bardic tale or idle boasting around a campfire, now it was frighteningly real and it was only skill and speed, bravery and luck, that mattered.

No sooner had the initial clash rung out and the screams of the maimed and dying were competing with the shock of steel upon steel than Adils, hidden all night in the woods, sprang forth with a ragged hardcore of followers bursting upon the English right like a horde of forest demons. Caught by surprise a flurry of English casualties resulted, including the noble Thorolf cut down by the traitor's blade.

Storming forward to avenge his brother's untimely fall Egil breathed fresh hope into the demoralised ranks and descended upon the triumphant renegades with the fury of revenge. This time there were few survivors left to flee back to the sanctuary of the woods, those who got that far were mercilessly hunted down amongst the trees that had earlier been their refuge but now became their graves.

The full fury of the main battle erupted over the plain at Wandon, warriors fell by the score but others stepped forward to replace them, the fertile banks became a butcher's yard, the green sward greased by the blood of many. All day the carnage lasted and only the setting sun dimmed the savage slaughter. By then, of course, it was decided — the Danish host was broken, hacked to bloody ribbons, its leaders anonymous corpses among the thousands, for the English it was indeed a great killing — a payment in full for all those earlier reversals at the hands of the Norsemen. The lessons of Carham and Battlebridge had been bloodily digested and brought to fruition by the banks of the Till.

Anlaf was slain and the remnants of his dismembered host pursued and harried across the breadth of the kingdom. A great victory for Northumbria, and for Athelstan, though even this momentous triumph has been overshadowed by the even more outstanding fight at Brunanburh for which so many sites, including Brinkburn, have been suggested.

The site of the battlefield is not marked upon the Ordnance Survey map but can easily enough be traced from the place names. Surprisingly, the site is some distance from Wandon and it seems as though the site of the Danish camp rather than the site of their destruction has given its name to history. Anyone sufficiently energetic to climb to the hill fort of Old Bewick can have a perfect northward view of the whole area.

'Select Fyrd' warrior with padded jerkin and helmet with nasal

'Great Fyrd' warrior — wearing essentially everyday clothes but with spear and shield.

Legend relates that there was an even earlier battle at Wandon fought shortly after the Saxons first came to the northern shore. Around 593 a descendant of Ida led a host from the infant kingdom of Bernicia to meet a Christianised Celtic king of Wales, named Caradoc, doutless in honour of his famous predecessor. Apparently the Welsh incursion was aimed at Christianising the heathen Saxon, no doubt with a suitably material reward in spoils. In any event the invaders were met at Wandon and thoroughly trounced, their Christianising monarch dispatched to join the ranks of unsung martyrs.

Old Bewick lies 3 to 4 miles east of Wooperton and can be reached via the A697 or B6346 from Alnwick via Eglinton.

Carham, 1018, NT833388.

The second battle of Carham was destined to be the last great battle on Northumbrian soil before the Norman conquest of 1066. It had a lasting significance in that it established the Tweed as the permanent border between England and Scotland, an effect which has survived to this day.

As has been noted the Earldom of Northumbria was much troubled by Scottish inroads, a difficult situation that was hardly alleviated by the conduct of Earl Waltheof, who preferred the safe sanctuary of his fortress at Bamburgh to the more hazardous business of active resistance.

In 1006 King Malcolm[1] and his Scottish host swept across the Tweed and laid waste, as was their wont, to large areas of the Earldom. Needless to say, they were largely unopposed as the Earl continued to prefer the safety of his coastal hold.

Encouraged by their so far easy passage the Scots pushed further, first as far as the Tyne and then, when the Earl still refused to budge, into Durham where they laid siege to the city itself. Outraged by his father's timorous indifference, Uctred, Earl Waltheof's offspring, determined to take matters into his own hands and rid the north of the Scottish pest.

Gathering a mixed levy from Durham and North Yorkshire he first raised the siege of Durham and then proceeded to drive the Scottish host back to the border. This swift and eminently successful campaign prompted King Ethelred to dismiss Waltheof and appoint Uctred Earl in his stead.

Flushed by his first wave of victories the new Earl began to make ample amends for his father's passive submission. The Scots were

[1] Not Shakespeare's Malcolm but an earlier namesake.

harried across their own borderland with such deadly intent that the Lothians were once again wrested back under the Northumbrian yoke.

Uctred's deeds had, inevitably, made him many enemies amongst lesser men, a list that quite possibly included the new sovereign, Canute. In any event Uctred was struck down by an assassin's blade in 1016 with the tacit, if not open, sanction of the king.

It was a bad day for the Earldom, for Uctred's brother Edwulf who was now appointed as Earl seemed cast more in his father's mould, quite prepared to forgo glory and ambition in the cause of life-expectancy. Edwulf's first act as Earl was to restore the Lothians to the Scots.

This may have gained him some friends north of the border but it only served to raise a storm of indignation further south. These vigorous protests originated from the Church, which in fact held vast tracts in the fertile Lothians and stood to lose considerable revenue if the land were permanently returned to Scotland's domain. To prevent the seemingly inevitable forfeiture of these estates the church militant girded itself for battle.

In order to tangle with the formidable Scottish host it was felt that a levy of all eligible males from Tyne to Tweed was needed, irrespective of age, infirmity, weapons or training. Convinced of the economic, if not the religious, need for this particular pecuniary crusade the vast unwieldy bulk of the Northumbrian army was hastened northward to meet, and hopefully chastise, the Scottish host.

This vast untrained force, looking less like an army than a peasant population on the move, tramping in dismal chaos across the Earldom, can hardly have suggested a Christian host bent on upholding the sacred cashflow of the church. The more experienced warriors doubtless prophesied disaster — they were entirely correct.

It was perhaps a fitting irony that the inevitable debacle should occur near the site of that earlier fight at Carham where the Vikings had made such a notable slaughter amongst the episcopacy. In fact, the clash actually took place roughly quarter of a mile north-west of the mound destined later to form the motte of Wark castle. Later castellans would have ample cause to rue the day that ever fixed the Tweed as the final boundary, as Wark was seldom absent from the copious annals of border warfare.

Malcolm's army must have seemed trim and deadly compared to the cumbersome dinosaur come to fight him. Another interested party was the Scottish warlord Owen the Bald, sometimes Lord of the Lothians, and therefore most interested in the day's sanguinary proceedings.

Details of the actual carnage have been lost but it seems to have been almost a carbon copy of the dismal, earlier fight against the Norsemen.

We can assume that most of the initiative came from the Scots, the English host reeling numbly before a concerted series of devastating hammer blows, that rent, and ultimately splintered, the already uneven ranks.

Predictably, the raw Northumbrian levies, who can hardly have had much fervour for their cause, could only stand so much and were soon in hopeless, headlong flight, leaving the Scots as complete masters of the field. For them it seems to have been an almost bloodless victory, and it was the men of Northumbria who were left to count the cost. We do not know how many lay stripped and naked, piled in the sacklike mounds of bloodied corpses, but the flower of the Earldom's nobility lay amongst them including, eighteen churchmen of note — one wonders how they contrived to write off that particular loss?

Only one significant result came of this particular abortive, profiteering crusade and that, as we have already noted, was the establishment of the River Tweed as the border between England and Scotland.

The area of Wark and Carham had already witnessed considerable blood-letting but was destined to see more when, in 1370, a third encounter took place in the vicinity.

Half a mile west of Wark at a spot known, appropriately, as Battle Place, English and Scots clashed again. In a typical border skirmish the Northumbrian contingent, under Sir John Lilburn, battled against a body of Scots led by Sir John Gordon. Though not by any means a major affair it was hotly contested, with the Scots faring badly. Despite repeated hammerings the Scots persisted doggedly, their tenacity so great that the English were eventually totally exhausted and forced to surrender to their stubborn foes. Northumbrians have never had any luck near Carham.

The site of the battle of 1018 is marked on the Ordnance sheet, though the date is incorrectly given as 1016. Carham is some miles west of Coldstream on the B6350 and the visitor is recommended to visit the remains of the castle at Wark whose scant traces do little justice to its role in border history.

Chapter Two

NORMAN, ENGLISHMAN AND SCOT

If I were stepping forward with one foot in paradise and the other still in my castle and someone sounded the call to battle, I would step backwards again.

The Tale of Garin of Lorraine

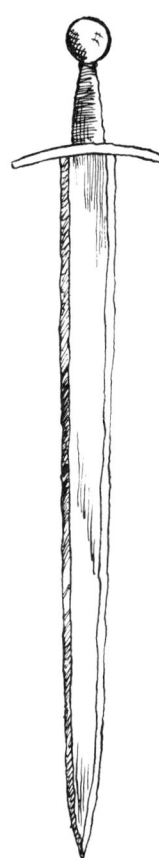

As every schoolboy knows 1066 was the year when it all happened, but even the crucial carnage on Senlac hill did not have immediate repercussions in the north. The long miles from the south served to dilute the effects of the present conquest much as they had done for earlier invasions.

At the outset the Conqueror and his son Rufus were content to maintain the Earldom of Northumberland, which remained, as ever, an effective buffer against the Scots. This policy however, proved fraught with risk, principally that of the 'overmighty subject' — a problem that arose on more than one occasion, in spite of such savage and salutory lessons as the wholesale slaughter and destruction wrought by William in 1080.

The rebellion of Robert Mowbray in the 1090's proved to be the final straw and the Earldom was abolished, the land being parcelled out amongst a larger group of magnates, thus avoiding the monopoly of power that the redundant Earls had wielded.

This policy of decentralisation was pursued further by Henry I, in whose reign the Granvilles gained the Barony of Ellingham, The De Umfravilles, Prudhoe and the De Vescis, Alnwick.

At last, the imprint of the Normans began to be felt in Northumberland as the new nobility began throwing up their distinctive Motte and Bailey castles — timber pallisades set upon earthen ramparts, to control and safeguard their new demesnes. Many of Northumberland's finest castles began life in this fashion, Harbottle, Mitford and Elsdon, the latter being one of the best preserved examples of the motte and bailey system in England.

Sword *c.* 1050.

An inevitable result of the spread of Norman influence was the introduction and expansion of the feudal system. Hereby, all grants of land came directly from the king to the barons or tenants in chief, the grant dependent upon military service. This process was repeated down the line as the barons parcelled out land to the knights, each of whom controlled his own manor. This was fine for those at the top, or in the upper echelons of the system, but it was less than benign towards those at the lower end, namely the serfs, who existed in a condition little improved on slavery, tied to the land as though by chains.

However, the overall number of Normans in Northumberland remained fairly small — some authorities rate their numbers, in the mid twelfth century, as only a few hundred, inclusive of families and personal retainers. Many of the older, indigenous Saxon nobility survived and learnt to swallow their already battered pride and accept the inevitability of the swaggering newcomers.

In any event, the Scots were a sufficient challenge to occupy the full attention of even the most battle hungry warlord. To describe the Scots as a 'problem' could rate as a single line summary of Anglo-Scottish border relations until the Union of the Crowns. What it means here is that they were more of a 'problem' than usual.

The dissensions and internecine strife of the early Norman period provided excellent scope for large scale forays and incursions. The most notable of these being the invasion of 1138 when a Scots army under David, their king, wreaked havoc through Northumberland on its southward route to a well-deserved Waterloo at Northallerton — the Battle of the Standard.

A truce in 1139 provided a welcome respite, though the Earldom of Northumberland was promised to the Scottish heir who was able to claim descent through Waltheof, of earlier notoriety. Henry II, however, found it expedient to renege on this claim in 1157 and maintained his refusal against William the Lion, a valiant and energetic monarch, who came to grief beneath the walls of Alnwick. His capture, surprisingly, heralded a new era of peace upon the borders, the like of which had scarcely been seen since the Eagles departed and would not be seen again for many a long year after.

Peace was to reign almost unchallenged for a century when Northumberland was able to enjoy a renaissance unparalleled since the bygone days of the Golden Age. Scotland too, was able to benefit and Berwick, then a Scottish city, boomed with the burgeoning of the wool trade — able to count her revenues in thousands, whilst Newcastle still counted hers in hundreds.

This unlikely spate of calm was brought to an end when Alexander III, King of Scotland, rode out in the dark, against his courtiers' advice and broke his neck in a fall. This was in 1286 and seldom has one ill-advised ride so hastened the swift and terrible transition from a century of peace to a welter of bloody carnage.

The heir to the Scottish throne was the infant Margaret, the maid of Norway, who was to be brought from Scandinavia to marry the equally young prince of Wales. The child did not survive the arduous sea crossing and thereby left a vacuum around the Scottish throne with various rival claimants already with hands upon sword hilts. Edward I of England stepped into the darkening maelstrom with a magnanimous offer of arbitration, his modest fee for the service being an oath of fealty from the chosen candidate. Balliol, no more than a puppet king, thus grovelled his way to a shaky throne, provoking a rash of hostilities from his proud countrymen, with whom the idea of an English marionette did not sit well.

Edward stormed northward to put his iron stamp on Balliol's tottering authority. Wark, which the Scots had captured, was retaken and Berwick was besieged, the proud Plantagenet contemptuously leaping the first defences and thereby unleashing a chain of violence that deluged Berwick in blood and ran rampant on the borders for centuries thereafter.

Raids, counter-raids, excursions and forays began almost at once and all helped to establish a dreary pattern of violence, and more violence, that was to leave an indelible imprint upon the history and character of the border and its inhabitants.

It was now that the ubiquitous reiver and mosstrooper crept into existence, plying their clandestine occupation with gathering ferocity until the kingdoms were finally united.

Both the redoubtable Wallace and the later, less romantic though more successful, Bruce mercilessly harried Northumberland and the marches, sweeping down with fire and sword, thrusting the full horrors of war back upon their English foes, rolling across the border like a steel tipped avalanche. The peace of the previous century vanished like the morning mist and only the memory growing steadily dimmer beneath the welling tide of blood remained.

From now on Northumberland was to become an embattled landscape, the gaunt, stone towers raising their blunt profiles across the moors and dales, castles, towers, peles and bastles[1] became the order of the day. Men with land and beasts needed stout spears and stouter walls to keep a grip on either.

As a result of these bloody days Northumberland can boast more fortified places than any other English county, ranging from the impressive might of the great coastal fortresses, Bamburgh and Dunstanburgh, with equally formidable holds inland at Alnwick, Warkworth, Wark, Etal, Ford, Norham, Harbottle, Prudhoe. Lesser

[1] The exact distinction between the terms 'Pele', 'Bastle' is not an easy one to define and the two are used together so frequently so as to be almost indistinguishable. See note at end of chapter.

41

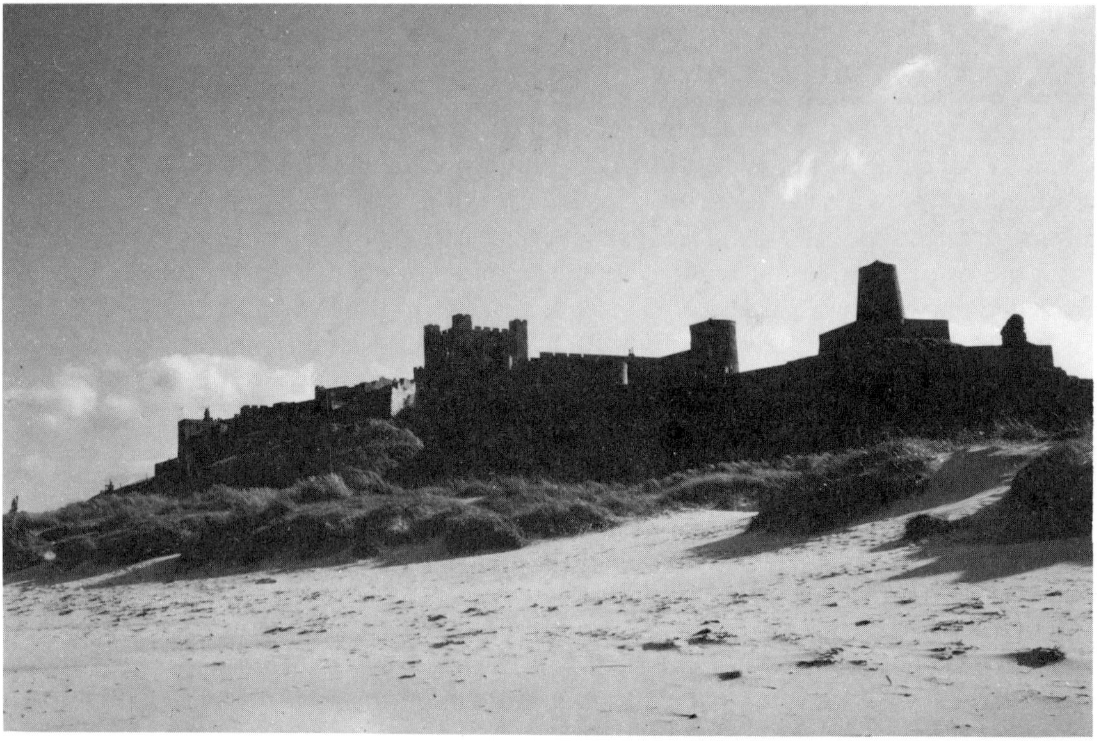

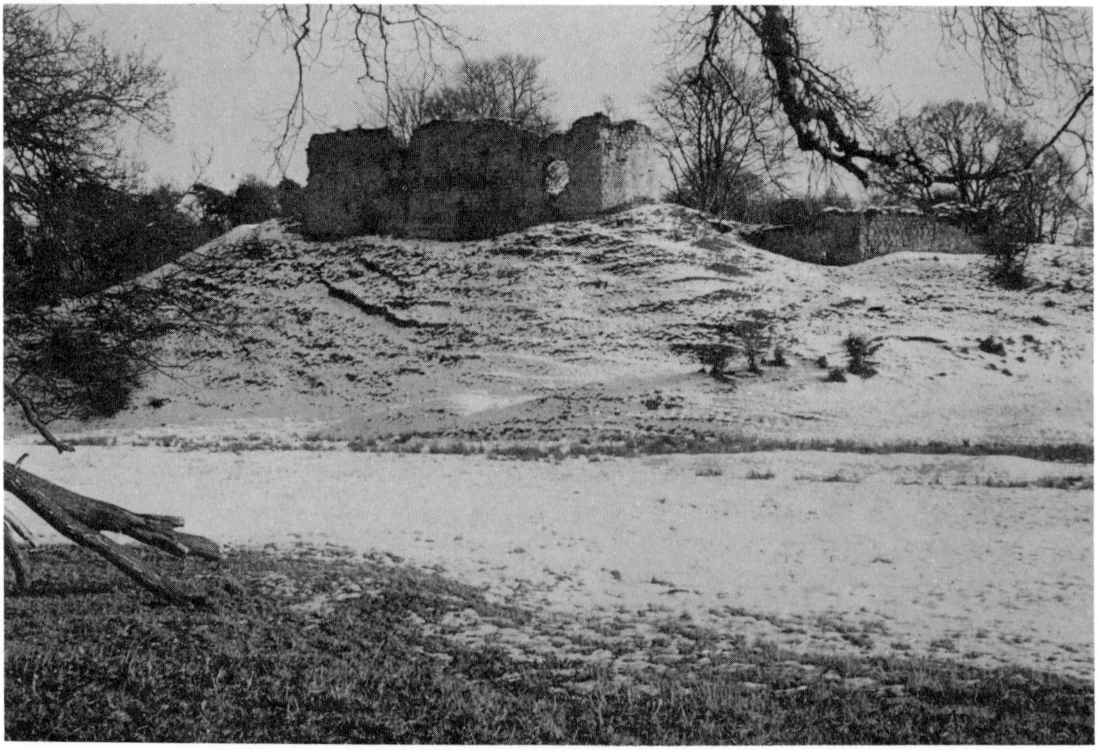

magnates built their fortified manors at Chipchase, Belsay, Aydon, Haughton and the rest. The list of peles is almost inexhaustible — Akeld, Gatehouse, Corbridge, Black Middings, to name but a very few.

Interspaced with all the major clashes and incursions were scores of lesser raids and skirmishes that could fill several volumes on their own. Many are undoubtedly unrecorded, perhaps not surprisingly, as men engaged in such desperate ventures are more apt to be concerned with their survival over the next few minutes, rather than their debt to posterity.

Several of the larger castles suffered considerably, especially those on the border itself — Norham was besieged almost continuously for two years in the early fourteenth century. Others such as Etal, Wark and Ford were badly knocked about, especially in the campaign of 1513 where heavy artillery was first used extensively. The need for defensible dwellings continued well into the sixteenth, and even into the early seventeenth centuries.

Even the development of artillery did not immediately render the border holds totally redundant as it had the majority of medieval castles — the harsh terrain, tractless wastes and rolling hills made the transport of the heavy guns a major undertaking at any time, almost impossible. As we have seen this did not deter James IV bringing his magnificent siege train with him en route to his gory Waterloo at Flodden. Even earlier, castles such as Dunstanburgh, had suffered terribly from bombardment by Yorkist forces during the Wars of the Roses.

The Medieval period was the heyday of the heavy cavalryman, the mounted knight, beloved of chivalric legend, whose main function in battle was to decide the issue with the shock impact of the charge. Meeting the mounted enemy head on, in the carnage of armoured collision, and then proceeding to ride down the ill-armed motley of feudal levies that fulfilled the distinctly secondary role of infantry.

These knights were descended from the host that followed Duke William across the English Channel and those who also survived the bloody slopes of Senlac. Theirs is a familiar image — clad in a shirt of fine mail or 'Byrnie' reaching to the calves, split front and rear so that the wearer might mount but still be able to afford at least some degree of protection to riders' vulnerable legs. This was of necessity a somewhat weighty item, averaging around thirty pounds and was not usually donned until combat appeared imminent. Protection to the head was afforded by a mail hood or 'coif' surmounted by a conical steel cap, or helm, finished with a straight nasal bar to guard against a slash at the face.

On his left side the horseman carried the distinctive kite shaped

Opposite:
Bamburgh on a basalt outcrop touching the cold North Sea; legend associates this ancient fortress with 'Joyous Garde' of Arthurian fame; was this truly where Lancelot and Guinevere fled?

Mitford Castle, largely ruinous though still impressive, and once the lair of the infamous Gilbert de Middleton, who terrorised Northumberland in the reign of King John and even dared kidnap the Bishop of Durham.

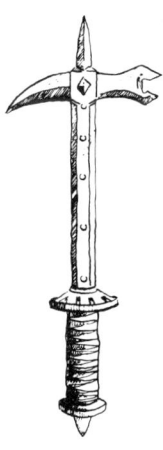

War-hammer
c. 1420.

shield, the arm slipped through the leather strap leaving the hand free to grip the reins. The right hand was left free and unencumbered so that the rider could wield his sword — one of the most important weapons in the knightly arsenal. Almost equally favoured for gentlemanly combat was the lance which, at this early stage, was kept fairly short and could be employed both for thrusting and as a missile.

The decisive victory of the mounted knight at Hastings established a supremacy that would last until the age of gunpowder, a supremacy that would even survive the onslaught of the longbow and the bill. It was not until the arrival of the first crude but deadly handguns, which even in the hands of an almost untrained and totally despised peasant levy could dispatch a round half dozen mounted men with no apparent regard for chivalry or social standing, that the knight was totally displaced. Until then he was the epitome of valour and martial glory, the true cutting edge of royal and baronial power alike.

Plate armour did not begin to supplant mail as the horseman's first line of defence until some time after the conquest. By the fourteenth century odd pieces of plate were being used as an additional protection to especially vulnerable areas. As the menace of the longbow increased the use of plate became extended and by the end of that century full plate armours were rapidly becoming the norm.

A full, well fashioned armour could easily weigh sixty pounds and though this may seem heavy it was far from being unsupportable, especially when distributed evenly around the torso and limbs. The popular vision of the armoured knight unhorsed, floundering, helpless and immovable is almost totally a misconception, especially since the wearer had been trained since early youth to move and fight in armour.

By far the greater menace was the risk of total exhaustion and even, in extreme circumstances, suffocation caused by the tremendous heat generated from within the confines of the armour — this was the factor to which the knights succumbed.

In medieval warfare the knights, professional retainers and men at arms constituted an elitist minority. The remaining bulk of armed forces being made up of peasant levies and bowmen, often little more than a rabble, untried and almost always unwilling, drawn by feudal obligation and the prospect of plunder. Their role in victory was little more than merely supportive, whilst in defeat they could expect to be ridden down without mercy by the enemy horsemen, whilst their own mounted superiors could either flee, or, if taken, could look forward to fair treatment and an eventual ransom. Generally, the paladins of chivalry extended the tenets of their code only to members of their own class, to whom warfare was not just an occasional occurrence, but more a way of life.

One effective answer to the rush of armoured knights was the Scottish pike formation or 'Schiltrom'. This was a compact, circular or square body of peasant infantry, each equipped with a stout twelve foot pike. Front ranks remained kneeling, ramming the butts of their pikes into the earth, whilst behind them, the second rank stood with weapons levelled at shoulder height and over the heads of those kneeling below and before. A charging foe was thus greeted with an impenetrable steel fanged hedgehog, a phenomenon that on several instances confounded the chivalric hosts of the English, most notably at Stirling Bridge, and then decisively at Bannockburn.

The hard fought clashes of the Scottish war of independence bred bitter knowledge. Bloody lessons, such as Falkirk, were not soon forgotten and Bruce, whose doughty pikes put paid to King Edward's magnificent host, evolved a simple but effective doctrine for the use of the schiltrom known as 'King Robert's Testament'. This basic treatise proposed that the spearman should always fight dismounted, arrayed upon the slope of a hill, flanked by either forestation or some equally impenetrable obstacle, such as a village or mire. This position should preferably be fronted by soft ground as well, so as to clog the momentum of the enemy's charge. The Scots, who led their host to awful decimation at Halidon Hill, should have paid closer heed to the great warrior's advices. Strangely enough, it was the position of the English at that engagement that bore most resemblance to the ideal expressed in the testament, though it was the longbow, rather than the pike, whose shafts cemented the certain doom of the reckless foe on that fatal field.

The pikeman's real enemy was the longbow — the inert densely packed ranks of the schiltroms formed superb static targets and almost every lethal shaft could be made to tell. It was the longbow that flayed the Scottish squares at Falkirk and transformed their shambling advance at Halidon Hill into a butcher's yard. Truly it was the bowmen of England who avenged the sad debacle of their knighthood at Bannockburn.

The redoubtable English longbow was indeed a fearsome weapon, capable of six aimed shots per minute. It was cheaper and lighter than the crossbow, though considerably more skill was required in the handling. Constant practice at the butts made the English masters of their weapons, able to draw back full to the ear creating a drawing weight of nearly seventy pounds on a six foot bow that would then dispatch a shaft as far as three hundred yards[1]. Even mail and plate

[1] In a trial made before Edward VI in 1550, arrows were shot through a one inch board of seasoned timber. The usual maximum range was 250 yards. In 1798, 1856, 1881 and 1897 ranges of 340, 308, 286, 290 and 310 yards were reached.

combined were no real protection and so even the full costly equipage of knighthood would not save the wearer. Although this threat had always existed from the powerful but generally scarce crossbow or arbalest, the short Norman bow, in general use until the introduction of the longbow, had been drastically lacking in this kind of hitting power.

Warfare at this period, like any other, was extremely unglamorous, it was also bloody, clumsy, brutal and often pointless, justified by nothing more than the urge to pillage, sanctified by a thin wash of knightly courtesy. Usually the issue was decided by the murderously savage onslaught of the charge and the deadly mêlée that followed. It was essentially a localised affair with none of the vicarious violence of modern warfare — sophisticated fire guidance systems or high altitude bombings, then the horrors were spread by more traditional means, fire and sword, rapine, slaughter and pillage. Often, then as now, it was not the combatants who suffered most but the indigenous inhabitants of all the border shires who could confidently expect that, to whosoever went the victory, theirs would be the loss. Crops destroyed, property burned, stock lifted, themselves either massacred outright or left to starve on the bitter fruits of devastation. Few of the major, or even minor, clashes described hereafter were not preceded and/or followed, by widespread depredation and looting. To the hapless folk, caught in the violent mesh of the borders dark centuries, it must indeed have seemed to them that they inhabited a mere jungle, and one that was overstocked with predators.

Apart from the outright fatalities from actual wounds, horrific gaping gashes from broadsword and axe, many only slightly wounded would have little hope of survival — medical facilities were almost non-existent and infections rampant. It was not unknown for some of the

Note:
It has been suggested that the term 'Pele' is derived from the latin 'Pilum' i.e. a stake or pallisade, connoting that the original structure was simply a stout timber enclosure wherein stock could be gathered as protection from predators — man or beast. At this early stage there was no refuge for humans within the structure, later a simple wooden shelter was erected so that humans might shelter also — this developed into a stronger, more permanent and more defensible hold, though still of timber construction. When the timber rotted, or as might happen all too often, fell victim to the attackers' fire the survivors, should there be any, and benefiting from their harsh experiences rebuilt in stone, thus the pele came into being with an outer wall of stone, now known as the 'Barmkin' to replace the earlier timbers.
'Bastle' is believed to owe its origin in the French 'Bastille' i.e. tower which perhaps implies that the bastle was built as it now appears, in stone, and not on the site of an earlier wooden structure.
In any event the two terms are now generally taken to mean the same thing, a double storey, stonebuilt, rectangular tower, with a pitched stone slated roof, walls of impressive thickness, a barrel vaulted ground floor (as proof against fire) where beasts were gathered and an upper floor reached by an outside stone stairway wherein the inhabitants might shelter.

lesser armed soldiery and bowmen to fight unclothed, in the hope of avoiding the infection from wounds being fostered by filthy garments.

This is not the world of Mallory or Scott, jousting knights and damsels in distress closeted in distant but cosy towers, here was only cold, sleet, rain and sudden death. This dark pageant was now and then enlivened by the odd flashes of spectacular daring and gallantry that were later to serve as the model and inspiration of the romanticists. The defeat and capture of William the Lion by the mere handful at Alnwick, the deeds of Hotspur, Douglas' last fight at Otterburn, here was the stuff of true heroic legend but once the odd fire was extinguished the darkness once again descended.

Durham (1069) and Gateshead (1081)

'The French had possession of the place of slaughter as God granted them because of the nation's sins'

Thus, the Anglo-Saxon Chronicle laconically records the demise of the Saxon epoch and the advent of the Normans — dour, tough and professional. None more typified the breed than the Conqueror himself.

'A hard man was the King
. . . . he was sunk in greed
And utterly given up to avarice . . . Alas! that any man should bear himself so proudly
And deem himself exalted above all other men
May almighty God show mercy on his soul
And pardon him his sins.'

After Hastings William moved fast to consolidate his advantage, at this time the north had escaped relatively unscathed. The Northumbrians, led by Earls Edwin and Morcar had avoided the slaughter on Senlac ridge, though they had suffered an earlier mauling from Hardrada's Norsemen at Fulford.

Having accepted the fealty of the north from Aethelwine bishop of Durham and from Edwin and Morcar who submitted at York, the King, in 1067, gave the earldom to Copsig, a former associate of the unlamented Tostig. This Copsig had a somewhat dubious record and, at the time of his appointment seems to have been supporting himself by piracy. It does appear that William may have thought that by elevating one of their own number he may have been succeeding in

The cutting edge
of the Conquest
— a Norman
knight dressed
for the conflict
with kite-shaped
shield and mail
hauberk.

placating the turbulent Northerners. If so, he was mistaken. Copsig began his career as Earl by attempting to remove the surviving member of the old Northumbrian line, Osulf, who however, proved too slippery a fish and a canny exponent of guerilla tactics. The climax to this internecine strife was reached when Osulf surprised Copsig and his retainers at a banquet in Newburn. Though he fled to sanctuary, Osulf cheerfully set fire to the church and the Earl was slain.

One of Copsig's problems had been his role as tax gatherer, never an enviable post, and the King's recurrent demands for 'geld' from his northern subjects proved a stimulus for rebellion. Copsig's successor was Cospatric, who seems to have been created in a similar mould. A tax levy in the Spring of 1068 again served as a focus for discontent, Edwin and Morcar led the rebellion, Cospatric obviously deemed it wise to swim with the tide and came out in support. The rebels were bolstered by promises of aid from Swein of Denmark and Malcolm Canmore. Nonetheless the coalition proved unable to withstand the Conqueror's fury, the revolt petered out and the erstwhile leaders, including Edgar the Atheling, fled to Scotland.

To consolidate his grip on the northern half of his realm the King built a castle at York and appointed Robert Fitz Richard as governor. To extend his writ beyond the Tees, William sent a force under Robert Comines to hold Durham. Aethelwine warned the arrogant Norman that the Northumbrians would not accept the casual barbarity and rapacity which, all too often, was the trademark of officialdom. Comines, dismissed these prophetic words and gave his soldiers, perhaps 700 in all, licence to plunder Durham.

The apparent lack of resistance lulled the invaders, who, by dusk were scattered throughout the city. This wanton lack of caution invited disaster and the Northumbrians were quick to oblige. Beacons from the surrounding hills summoned warriors to muster outside the gates. At dawn the attack was launched.

Unable to regroup or consolidate any defensible position the Normans blundered through the narrow streets, assailed on every side, casualties mounted. The survivors, led by Comines, managed to barricade the Episcopal House where the Norman had earlier established his headquarters. After a desperate defence the remaining few were forced out as the house burnt. None survived.

The debacle at Durham was the signal for a more general rising, which quickly spread to engulf York — Fitz Richard, the castellan, perished in an ambush but the depleted garrison held out. Cospatric and The Atheling returned from Scotland. A relieving force of Norman Knights proved unable to proceed beyond Allerton:—

'It was rumoured that they had been struck with immobility by a supernatural force through the power of a saint named Cuthbert who was interred at Durham and protected the place of his repose . . .'

A less prosaic explanation is that the Normans, in unfamiliar territory, and beset by fog, feared another ambush. Again it was left to the King to galvanise his Knights into action. Moving with characteristic speed he confronted the rebels in the streets of York and forced them into flight. After the city had been made to feel his wrath, he strengthened the existing defences and appointed one of his most able subordinates, William Fitz Osbern, as castellan. 'He plundered the borough and made St. Peter's Church an object of scorn and also plundered and humiliated all the others;' (Anglo-Saxon Chronicle). Losing no time Fitz Osbern moved against the rebels and scattered their forces.

In the Autumn of 1069 Swein of Denmark dispatched a fleet of 240 ships commanded by his brother, Osbeorn. The Danish force included marauders from Poland, Saxony and Frisia but their invasion amounted to little more than a large scale foray, such as their forefathers had led. Nonetheless their arrival put new heart into the rebels and after a desperate battle their combined forces gained control of York though at a cost of the city's almost total destruction. Thus deprived of a power base the cause of these unlikely allies flagged and the initiative once again passed to the King who harried the invaders, penned them in and then bought them off.

William now decided that he had had quite enough of his northern subjects periodic outbursts and in his inimitable and utterly chilling manner devised a 'final solution' to the northern problem. The Normans began the systematic harrying of the region, carrying fire and sword through the Yorkshire dales, peasants slain, crops and steadings, even implements burnt, stock lifted. As the holocaust advanced to the Tees Cospatric hurried to submit. Durham was deserted, all who could had fled, but the scorched earth policy was continued through the county, to the Tyne and beyond, as far west as Hexham. This carnage produced the desired effect, famine and pestilence spread in its wake, desperate villagers even sold themselves into slavery simply to escape.

'. . . the end of liberty according to the English, of rebellion according to the Normans. On both sides of the Humber, the cavalry of the foreign King, his courts, his bailiffs and his courtiers, thenceforward travelled unmolested on the roads and through the towns; famine, like a faithful companion of the conquest, followed their footsteps.'

William was able to enjoy the peace his devastation had engendered until 1075. In that year a further rebellion broke out led by Earl Waltheof who had replaced the turncoat Cospatric. Initially he must have seemed like a good choice, the youngest son of the redoubtable Siward he had enjoyed the conqueror's favour and had been permitted the signal honour of marrying within the royal family. Taxation seems to, once again, have been the spark and Waltheof invited the Danes to join him. Again, however, the King moved too fast and the rebels were confounded. Split by internal strife the Danes could supply no more than a token force and the much strengthened defences of Durham proved impervious to their attack. A timber motte had been erected after the disaster of 1069 but this was rebuilt in stone in 1072, (at this time the cathedral building was that constructed in 998, the familiar Norman Cathedral was not begun until 1093).

The revolt fizzled out and Waltheof, for his treachery was thrown into gaol after submitting. The next actor on the stage was Walcher of Lorraine who had been made bishop of Durham in 1071. After the Waltheof rebellion he was able to purchase the Earldom thus adding secular to temporal wealth. Walcher's character remains a matter of dispute but of his greed and ambition there can be little doubt. Among his counsellors was Ligulf, connected by birth to the old Northumbrian line, and who became increasingly critical after a Scots incursion in 1079, during which Walcher seemed smitten by impotence. A feud arose between Ligulf and two of the Earl/Bishop's henchmen, his chaplain Leobwin and kinsman, Gilbert. Acrimony soon led to bloodshed with Ligulf and his household butchered.

In order to dampen the fuse of incipient rebellion Walcher agreed to meet with Ligulf's clan at Gateshead. There now seems little doubt that this proposed reconciliation was a trap laid by Eadulf Rus, leader and spokesman for the Saxons since the murder of Ligulf. All the same Walcher was taking no chances and had at least 100 retainers to support him. The Saxons presented a petition of wrongs but, according to legend, the arrogant Norman refused to consider these until he was paid £400. Rus retired, ostensibly to consult, but, in fact, to give the signal for attack 'Stout rede, good rede' was the cry as the Northumbrians fell upon the startled company. Walcher sought refuge in a church but the Saxons torched the roof, forcing the survivors out. Leobwin perished in the flames, Gilbert and the bishop were cut down as they sought to flee. The entire company was put to the sword, save, it is said, for two English retainers.

The rebels moved on to attack Durham but the siege faltered after four days and this final spark of northern resistance burnt itself out as before. The construction of strongholds such as the motte at Durham was a formidable bulwark against insurrection. Adequately provisioned a small garrison could hold out against vastly superior local forces. Fire was an obvious weapon against the early timbered castles though the defenders could counter this by draping wet hides over the pallisades. A stone keep demanded far more specialised siege machines and sophisticated mining techniques — resources that were beyond the means of local insurgents.

After the fracas of 1081 William resorted to his well tried tactic of laying waste the area, sending his half brother Odo to perform the necessary chore. Odo proved enthusiastic and the bitter harvest of 1069 was reaped once more. The chronic weakness of the Northumbrian cause was the absence of real leadership and motivation — most uprisings were sparked by a particular outrage and once that was avenged lacked a coherent cause.

Great Seal of William the Conqueror.

The Battle of Alnwick, 1093, NU193145.

In the winter of 1093 Malcolm Canmore, King of Scotland, that same Malcolm who had earlier vanquished Shakespeare's Macbeth, brought an army across the border in a large scale foray and laid waste to much of Northumberland. This was not the first time that the Northern Shire had quailed beneath the might of the warrior king, but this time would be once too often.

The excuse for the present incursion is said to have been Malcolm's pique for the shoddy treatment he had received at the court of the conqueror's son, William Rufus, when he went there to pay homage for his English estates.

Once the necessary justification had been established the Scots were free to set about the serious business of the campaign, sweeping through the northern half of the country like a scourge. By the time of the first frosts in November, Malcolm's hosts were leaguered beneath the walls of Alnwick. As the well practised grip of the besiegers tightened around the defences, the situation of the garrison soon became desperate.

Their only hope for deliverance lay in the person of Robert de Mowbray, Earl of Northumberland and governor of Bamburgh, whose forces were nevertheless totally inadequate to face the full weight of the Scottish host in open battle. In spite of this crippling disparity in numbers the Norman Earl determined to muster a striking force to attempt the relief of Alnwick.

This possibility seems to have eluded the Scots, who appear to have been caught totally by surprise when the English knights fell upon them in a savage battle before the ramparts of Alnwick, on St. Brice's Day, (13th November).

The date proved more than merely unlucky for Malcolm Canmore, as both he and his son Edward fell beneath the Norman lances. The spot where the royal pair met their sanguinary ends was adjacent to a well, known thereafter as 'Malcolm's Spring'. The legend of Malcolm's demise is that he was slain by one Hamund, a constable of Eustace de Vesey. The story relates that the Englishman rode boldly into the Scottish camp with the keys of Alnwick castle suspended from the tip of his lance. This ploy obviously succeeded in convincing the Scots that the castle was on the point of capitulation. Eager to clench so great a prize the Scottish Monarch dashed, unarmoured, from his tent to seize the keys from the very tip of Hamund's lance.

As his quarry emerged in innocent haste the Norman levelled his deceiving lance and spurred forward. As Harold fell at Hastings so did Malcolm at Alnwick, pierced through the eye and killed instantly.

Before his dismayed subjects could recover from their surprise the slayer had wheeled about and galloped back to the safety of the walls, bursting through the ranks of Scottish foot, who stood, seemingly paralysed, by the shock of their so unexpected loss. His escape involved a daring plunge into the swollen waters of the Aln; inevitably this stretch of water became known as 'Hamund's crossing'.

Whether this bold adventure actually occurred cannot be definitely ascertained, it stands like so many others in the alluring twilight where legend and history meet, an area which provided a living for romantic writers from the days of the bards onwards.

Whatever the immediate cause of his demise the King of Scots was slain and the leaderless mass of Scottish host foundered beneath the English onslaught, like some great headless beast, and scattered homeward in ignominious defeat.

The mortal remains of Malcolm Canmore and his son were interred in Tynemouth monastery by the grace of the victorious English. A footnote to the legend of his fall relates that the knight Hamund, was ever after known as 'Pierce eye' from his exploit. Another legend ascribes his nickname as the origins of the house of Percy — this, of course is totally untrue.

A rude stone memorial was shortly erected at the spot roughly·a quarter of a mile uphill from Malcolm's Well. This was replaced by a more sophisticated monument erected by the Duchess of Northumberland in 1774. The monument can still be seen, though largely obscured by trees, on the right hand side of the former route of the A1, reduced to a quiet lane by the bypass. Driving past the castle and over the river the site is at the top of the rise before the roundabout — the view of river and castle repay the effort.

The Battle of Alnwick, 1174.

Besieging Alnwick was to prove a dangerous diversion for members of the Scottish monarchy, one had fallen there already and another, cast in the same warlike mould, was also destined to come to grief.

This was William the Lion, whose rampant banner had been seen above the marches before, in 1172, when he had championed the cause of Henry II's rebellious brood. This first incursion came to naught however, and a hastily patched truce provided a lull that lasted for two years.

When William came again he was determined upon greater things than any mere raid. Bolstered by a hardcore contingent of Flemish mercenaries the swollen Scottish host was said to number eighty thousand, undoubtedly a considerable exaggeration but nonetheless a formidable army.

Inevitably, Northumberland suffered terribly as the Scottish host ravaged the Northern county, equally predictable, was the almost total lack of any real military triumph the expedition was able to achieve. Repulsed at Prudhoe, the Scots fell back to the banks of the Aln where they invested the town.

Sheer weight of numbers made the Scottish host a difficult creature to control, feudal armies were apt to be unwieldy at the best of times and William had divided his force into three marching columns. This was also a more satisfactory arrangement for the widespread pillaging which continued with a vengeance.

The easternmost prong of the host, commanded by Duncan of Fife, fell upon Warkworth with the voracity of starving locusts, pausing only to fire the church of St. Lawrence, crammed with helpless refugees most of whom, predictably, perished in the conflagration.

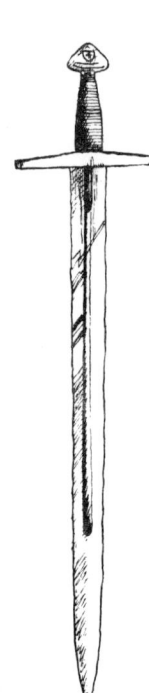

Sword *c.* 1150.

54

With fatal arrogance William could not foresee any serious challenge to so mighty a host and thus neglected to draw his scattered contingents around him at his base near Alnwick. Like many others before and after he forgot the old soldiers adage 'March divided, Fight united' — an omission for which he was to pay dearly.

Unknown to William, not quite all of Northumberland's garrisons were content to remain behind the shelter of citadel ramparts — on the night of 11th July a party of some four hundred mounted knights had left Newcastle and headed north. This diminutive band was led by Ranulph de Glanville and included Bernand Balliol and Robert de Stuteville with several other notable and seasoned warriors, sons of the men who had blunted the great Scottish host beneath the banners of the saints of Northallerton.

The northward ride continued throughout the night and into the mists of early dawn, determined somehow to strike a blow at the ravaging horde of Scots. A picked force of volunteers bent upon a desperate and dangerous adventure, the very stuff of chivalry, that could easily have been lifted from the pages of Walter Scott or G. A. Henty.

Riding by moonlight, the crisp night air alive with the soft creaking of harness and the jingle of spurs, the miles steadily slipped away. The steady transition from darkness to dawn obscured by the twisted shroud of the mist that lay around them, providing an impenetrable cloak to their approach, and deadening the giveaway rattle of hoofbeats.

As if by some unseen alchemy the mist was suddenly gone and the towers and ramparts of Alnwick loomed before them, bathed in the clear radiance of the early morning sun.

Directly in their path, in a meadow beneath the walls, there was a banner fluttering proudly in the breeze, the unmistakable motif of the lion rampant left no doubt as to whose camp they had arrived at.

Tired men, snapped upright in the saddle, fatigue routed by a sudden tensing, palms that were suddenly clammy closed upon sword hilts, fronted shields, levelled lances. Nervous horses, sensing the sudden change, fretted at the bit, but the uncertainty was to be shortlived. Orders rapped out through the clear air, spurs were dug and the calm of the morning fled from the clatter of drumming hooves.

The cluster of pavilions that had proclaimed the presence of the King of Scots suddenly erupted into life. Secure in the daunting legions of his host William had camped surrounded by nothing more than his own immediate retainers, no more than sixty fighting men at most. Leaping from his warrior's couch at the first shout of alarm, he burst forth into the dawn to see a cloud of horsemen descending upon his encampment. At first, he thought the force might come from his own host but the speed of their advance belied any such fond illusion. King William and his bodyguard threw on their mail and clambered into the saddle.

Notwithstanding the absolute surprise the English had achieved the Scots were still able to meet the charge head on, a milling explosion of armoured men and heavy horses. The mêlée, stamping, cursing, clashing, shrieking carnage was ended almost ere it began. William's mount was killed beneath him; unhorsed, and winded, the Lion's roar subsided and he was compelled to submit to the ring of levelled lances. Outnumbered, and now leaderless, his surviving followers likewise laid down their arms.

William the Lion was brought back captive to Newcastle, his mighty host reeled and foundered with the loss and dissipated northward leaving the harassed Northumbrians safe to count the cost.

The capture of the King of Scots came at a most convenient moment for Henry II, who, at the time was doing penance for procuring the demise of his erstwhile Archbishop, Thomas a' Becket. Such a stroke was certain proof that the saints were appeased and it was equally certain that any future royal invader would think twice before planting his standard before the walls at Alnwick.

Norham 'The Queen of Border Fortresses', scene of Scott's *Marmion*. Its walls defied the Scots till the age of artillery.

56

The Battle of Halidon Hill, 1333, NT872548.

Following the decimation of the English chivalry at Bannockburn, Northumberland was left, once again, to savour the bitter fruits of a Scottish victory. In 1318 Bruce was able to take control of Berwick, albeit with the collusion of several of the garrison. Constant inroads harried the Marches whilst the King of England, Edward II, remained indifferent, stung into total impotence by his catastrophic defeat. Finally, in 1327, Edward was at first deposed and then horribly murdered by his estranged Queen and her ambitious lover Roger Mortimer. The new ruler was the fourteen year old Edward III, who soon threw off the tenuous shackles of Mortimer's influence, that gentleman's next and final journey being to the block.

The following year Edward negotiated a treaty with Scotland known as the 'Shameful Peace' whereby he agreed to renounce all claim to the Scottish throne — a bargain to be sealed by the marriage of Edward's sister to the young prince David. It appeared that some form of lasting peace had at last been effected and the young bride was christened the princess 'Make-Peace'.

These hopes were dimmed when Bruce died shortly afterwards, leaving a regency council in control of the realm. The worthy councillors became increasingly alarmed over a condition of the peace which stipulated that those estates sequestered from Scottish nobles previously allied to England should be returned. On paper this condition did not appear altogether unreasonable if, as indeed it seems, the old grudges were to be forgotten. In reality the Scottish nobility were considerably less than willing to welcome old enemies back into the fold, especially when these included Edward Balliol, son of the infamous 'Toom Tabard'. Their fears over this individual's ambitions proved well grounded, the great Bruce was scarcely cold when the erstwhile renegade boldly laid claim to the crown, a challenge that the wily young king of England was quick to support.

Balliol's early efforts met with some success, the regent Moray fell in battle and the usurper was actually able to gain the throne, though not before he had sworn homage to his Royal English patron. This final degredation was too much for the hardy Scots, who had suffered too long to win their independence, and a swift rebellion parted Balliol from his uncertain sceptre. Ignominiously, he scuttled southward and appealed to Edward for aid.

Angered at the summary expulsion of his vassal, the King of England resolved that his northern neighbours should be thoroughly chastised, a decision of which his formidable grandfather would have no doubt heartily approved.

The first stage of the campaign was to be the investiture of Berwick. This was a movement the Scots had hardly failed to anticipate, consequently they had strengthened and provisioned the garrison, which was more than ready to withstand a lengthy siege.

In February 1333 the first of the English troops, led by Sir William Montague, arrived to begin the siege. Due to their extensive preparations the Scots easily repulsed several early attempts at an escalade. Despite these setbacks the English were able to disperse a French squadron lying offshore and establish a firm blockade.

By the time Edward himself appeared before the walls in May the agonies of a protracted siege were already making themselves felt upon the inhabitants. Apart from the constant alarums and the battering of various siege engines, the besieged had to endure such subtle tactics as having the rotting carcases of animals catapulted over the defences in the hope of spreading disease.

Horseman's axe
c. 1200.

As a diversion from the tedium of such a protracted siege Edward encouraged his forces to pillage far and wide throughout the Lothians. By 15th July the situation of the garrison was desperate and, according to custom, the governor, Seton, agreed that if a relief force did not arrive within five days (i.e. by 20th July), then Berwick would capitulate. As a pledge of good faith Seton sent the elder of his sons to join the younger as an additional hostage in the English camp.

Edward had by now, however, received fresh intelligence that Sir Archibald Douglas, the new regent, was massing a formidable host for the relief of Berwick, a host that was even now poised to descend upon Northumberland.

The intention of the Douglas was to by-pass Berwick and feint toward Bamburgh, where Edward's queen was resident, in the hope that the threat would be sufficient to prise the English King away from the walls of Berwick. Edward was far too clever to be fooled by such a ruse — the citadel of Bamburgh was more than proof against such a hasty onslaught and he knew that his lady was safe.

Edward was, nonetheless, concerned that the Scottish host might still be formidable enough to seriously embarrass his army at Berwick. Consequently, he issued an appalling threat to the garrison that, unless they surrendered immediately, both of the young hostages would die.

This particularly barbarous piece of blackmail was not successful and in the event that the Scots may have felt the threat to be a mere bluff, the anxious Seton was awarded the heart-rendering spectacle of seeing both of his ill-fated boys hanged before the beleaguered walls, supposedly at the spot known appropriately as 'Hang-A-Dyke-Neuk'.

They kennt the tread o' their gallant bairns,
As they cam forth to die
Richard he mounted the ladder fyrst,
And threw himself frae the tree.

William he was his mithers pride,
And he looked sae bauldly on:
Then kissed his brothers lyefless hands,
When he found the breath was gane.

He leaped from off the bitter tree,
And floutchered in the wynd:
Twa bonnie flowers to wither thus,
Nd a' for yae mans mind.

After the hangings, which served no real purpose other than to convince the Scots of Edward's ruthless intent, something which they had probably never doubted, the siege continued much as before without any serious interference from the Scots army. Douglas, having failed to lure Edward away from Berwick, retreated to Duns to ponder upon a fresh initiative.

The mere presence of a Scottish host so near at hand was considered sufficiently serious for Edward to leave the siege in the care of a mere token force, whilst removing the rest of his army to a more suitable vantage.

The slopes of Halidon Hill, some two miles north-west of Berwick rise some six hundred feet above sea-level. The gradient is by no means severe, and in fact, the present day road, the A6105, nearly bisects the fatal slope.

The position that Edward had chosen shows how well he had digested the bitter lessons of his father's bloody nose at Bannockburn and how well he understood the victor's pragmatic 'testament'. On one flank the English were protected by a wood and at the base of the hill, by a mire.

Apart from the tactical differences, the English army of Halidon Hill was rapidly becoming a different, and altogether more professional, creature to that which had foundered at Bannockburn. The men who stood upon that slope were of the same stamp as those who would spread havoc throughout the realm of France during the bitter carnage of the Hundred Years War.

The feudal host was a clumsy, reluctant and unwieldy machine though, as far back as the reign of Henry II, some early attempts at reorganisation had been made. The Assize of Arms of 1181 had sought to regulate the arms and equipment to be carried by each of the differing social classes who went to form the host. That formidable monarch Edward I, redoubtable grandfather of the present king, had continued this reforming trend with the Statute of Winchester whereby five main categories of fighting men were determined. A knight, obviously in the higher oders, had to provide his own mount, arms and armour, whereas those at the lower end of the scale were required to bring only a bow and a quantity of arrows. This meant that a mounted knight could expect to incur considerable capital outlay merely in equipping himself for the field. Furthermore, a condition of the statute provided for the fining of any landowner whose estate was valued in excess of twenty pounds per annum and who shirked the call of knighthood. Thus chivalry became compulsory.

These provisions would provide the king with the iron clad heart of any army, though for the rest he had either to rely upon the feudal levy or on the employment of mercenaries. The latter were not only expensive but were likely to be viewed with some suspicion by the barons who perpetually feared that the hired lances could be turned against them. Indeed, their concern was such that a provision in Magna Carta had sought to discourage the king from engaging such swords for hire.

If the king could not procure mercenaries then he could always arrange to pay his own troops, this, in effect, created the beginning of pecuniary reward rather than feudal obligation. Again, of course, this method was still expensive but by the mid fourteenth century had become commonplace.

The usual mode of recruitment was for the monarch to place 'contracts' with leading captains who undertook, under the terms of their individual agreement, the responsibility for raising troops, i.e. so many, knights, men-at-arms and archers.

This all involved a considerable cash outlay but, hopefully, the investment would return a handsome bonus from ransom and booty if the campaign succeeded. The taking of valuable prisoners was big business in itself. Edward received something in the order of £268,000.00 in ransom money between 1360-70. Though the ransom traditionally belonged to the particular captor it invariably ended up by being shared out between king and captain. Often the individual was left with only a fraction of his prisoner's actual worth.

It was at this time also that the true potential of the longbow was becoming more fully realised. The short bow had been in use ever since the Conquest, as had the crossbow, always favoured by mercenary units but never popular here outside of a purely defensive role.

Brass of Sir
William Fitzralph
c. 1323 in
Pebmarsh
Church, Essex.

The longbowmen of Wales inflicted numerous casualties upon Edward I's conquering chivalric horde but once the valleys and mountains were finally subdued the king lost little time in adding drafts of Welsh archers into his own ranks.

A longbowman had but little of the protective hardware worn by the knight, his body armour was limited at best to a mail shirt topped by a coif and a simple iron skull or kettle hat. His true defence lay in his expertise with the bow, a skill that required years of constant practice, arm and shoulder muscles developing almost to the point of deformity.

Ordnances were passed to make practice at the butts compulsory, a form of encouragement that even went so far as to excuse any accidental slaying in the course of practice, almost literally a 'licence to kill'.

The actual weapon was usually about five feet in length, yew being the favoured timber though others, ash, elm or wych hazel were not unknown. The shaft, flighted with feathers from duck or peacock, was over a yard in length, 'the cloth yard shaft' and was tipped with a needle pointed steel pile. The string was drawn back to the ear, rather than only to the chest as with the short bow, thus the penetrating power of the delivered shaft was truly terrifying, capable, as we observed earlier of punching through as much as four inches of oak.

Edward did not have long to wait, over thirteen thousand Scottish spears with eleven hundred odd horsemen were soon advancing along the road from Duns. As always, the foot would rely on the solid phalanx like formation, the schiltrom, that had served them so well at Bannockburn, but the two decades that had elapsed since that resounding victory had produced a very different enemy.

The Scots commander and his fellow peers had drastically underrated the new strength and characteristics of their foe, Douglas, with all the near quixotic elan of his tribe, was about to commit his army to a major confrontation without pausing to evaluate, either the terrain, or the opposition, an outlook that formed a sad contrast to Edward's cool and deadly professionalism. The Scots were as tough, courageous and determined as ever but their tactics were sadly out of date.

On the 19th July the Scottish advance upon Berwick began with the host split into four marching columns. The first was commanded by John, Earl of Moray, with Sir John and Sir Simon Fraser, the second was under the nominal leadership of the young monarch though the actual command was vested in Sir James Stuart. The Douglas himself commanded in the third column along with the Earl of Carrick, whilst Hugh, Earl of Ross led the fourth.

Half a day's march from the village of Lamberton brought the

English longbow-
man mid 14th
Century.

tramping cohorts within site of the enemy's vantage, which, even at such a distance, must have been a daunting prospect. The English were already drawn up in order of battle, their knighthood dismounted and placed in compact bodies standing between the longbow formations, one wing of Edward's army was commanded by the hated Balliol himself.

Douglas at least had sufficient sense to reason that any attempt to pass by the English position whilst remaining strung out along the road in marching order would be folly in the extreme. Consequently, he decided upon a wide flanking movement that, hopefully, would serve both to keep his men immune from the lethal deluge of the English archers and might also tempt them into a precipitate onslaught, away from their present secure positions.

The ground across which Douglas proposed to launch his advance appeared to be perfectly level, indeed this was so, unfortunately it was also a swamp, a factor that did not become apparent to the Scots until they had, in fact, descended into it. As the marching columns began to flounder in the quaking mass underfoot, horse and foot inevitably became intermingled, bodies of pikemen collided in the morass, soon, inevitable confusion reigned supreme.

This sudden and altogether unexpected setback had tried Douglas's slim concept of generalship to the limit and with his army wallowing in a totally disorganised chaotic mess he could see only one route away from the debacle; an immediate frontal assault.

Painfully, slowly, the mass of Scots began to surge forward toward the English position, confused and disorientated already, before they had sustained a single casualty, though casualties there would presently be, and in abundance.

Seldom had the English longbowmen been blessed with such a gift, an almost perfect target laid out like a sacrifice below them and almost immediately the slaughter began. Volley after volley flashed and thudded home into the close packed ranks, doing fearful execution amongst the hapless spearmen. So dense was the press that scarcely a single shaft failed to find a mark, men went down in droves, thrashing in agonised, bloodied bundles as the hardened steel bit rendingly into flesh and bone.

Bannockburn had taught the English respect for the pike the Scots had now to learn proper respect for the longbow.

Doggedly the ravaged host plodded uphill free at last from the sucking tendrils of the morass, but lashed ever harder by the cloth-yard storm that sped and spitted into the struggling mass, taking a dreadful toll of noble and peasant alike.

In a welter of dead and dying, the ragged ranks faltered and the dragging onslaught foundered beneath the incessant deluge. This was the moment — with a savage cheer of exultation the English broke formation and swept down, like troops of hungry wolves upon the exhausted and depleted Scots.

For a while the doughty pikes held the avalanche at bay, the irresistible wave lapping around the slender shore. Until, amid the clangour and chaos of the fight, the line broke and the tide of battle flooded down the corpse-strewn slope, the summit the Scots had striven so hard to reach receding forever behind the rout.

The slaughter now was truly dreadful, the fleeing Scots were harried for a full five bloody miles amply charted by the heaps of their slain. By the end of the day the slopes of Halidon had cost the Scots four thousand dead, including Douglas himself, who did not live to see the full enormity of his blunder. With him, lay the Earls of Ross, Carrick, Lennox and Atholl, not till the holocaust at Flodden would the Scots know such a dreadful loss again.

For the English the stain of Bannockburn had finally been expunged and the tactics that won at Halidon were to strike again and again, at Crècy, Poitiers and Agincourt and earn for the fearful English longbowmen an everlasting reverence in the annals of war. In fact, the battle had cost the English few casualties. Some had fallen in the clash but once the ranks had broken the Scots were too demoralised to inflict any further damage and had no thought left but for flight:- 'making use of their heels but the English pursued them on horseback, felling the wretches with iron shod maces'.

Legend relates the tale of a bizarre and unequal duel fought prior to the main engagement, a combat in the best traditions of David and Goliath. Before the Scots advanced a massive Scottish warrior named Turnbull, accompanied by an equally large bull mastiff, strode forward and boldly challenged any Englishman who dared to stand forth from the ranks and fight.

Not altogether unsurprisingly there was hardly a rush to engage the fearsome pair. At last, rather than see his comrades shamed, a young knight of Norfolk, Sir Robert Benhale, took up the gauntlet.

Both sides watched eagerly as the oddly unmatched combatants circled and struck. First the huge mastiff pounced upon the slender youth, who neatly split the mutt, disembowelled by the force of its own rush. Next, it was the master's turn and a savage combat ensued, but the giant's brawn could not avail against the speed and skill of his younger adversary and the encounter ended abruptly as the Scotsman's head rolled upon the heather.

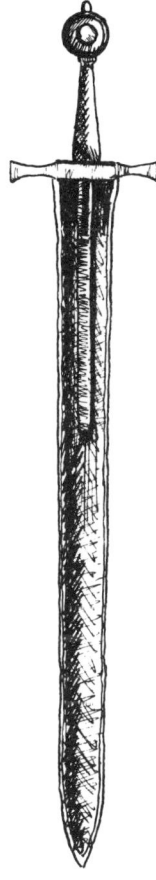

Sword *c*. 1300.

Scots out of Berwick and out of Aberdeen, at the Burn of Bannock
ye were far too keen
King Edward has avenged it now, and fully too I ween.

As mentioned the site can be viewed by the motorist from the A6105
some 3 miles N.W. of Berwick, though the road cuts across the slope
and the low lying ground has now been drained it is possible to get a fair
impression of the lie of the land as it was in 1333.

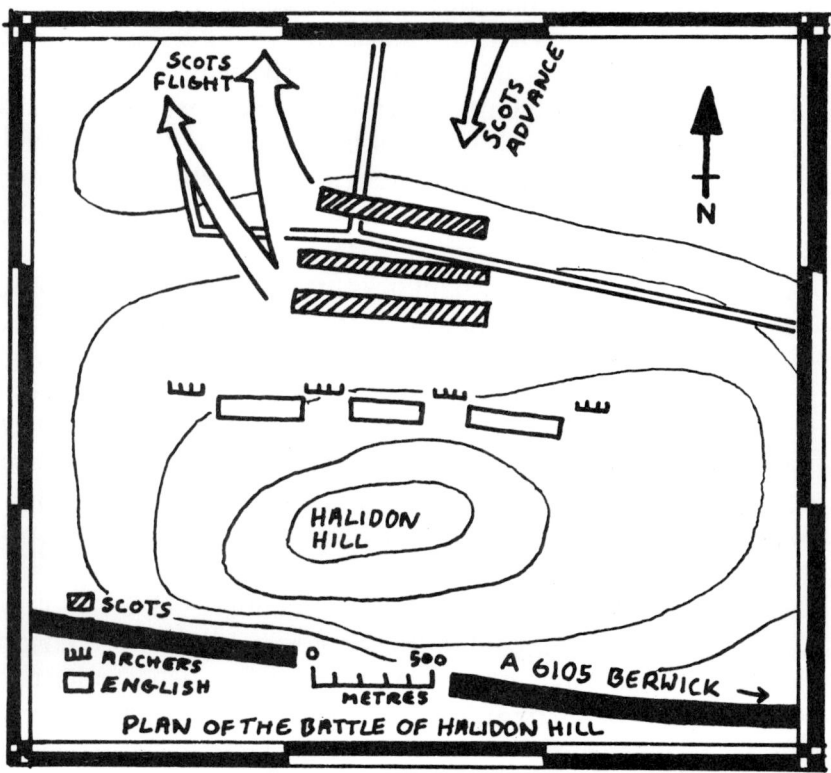

Nevilles Cross, 17th October, 1346.

Though Halidon Hill was a major blow to the Scots it did not end the
cycle of cross border strife, the Scots were too tough to be cowed by a
single defeat, however great. By the end of the decade, Edward III had
found that bashing his northern neighbours was far less profitable than
bashing those across the Channel and by 1340 the English were
becoming increasingly committed in France. In 1346, at Crecy, the
English scored a spectacular triumph and ever increasing tracts of
French soil came under their control. David II of Scotland had been
exiled in France after the debacle at Halidon and only returned in 1341.
Increasingly despondent at the unbroken run of English victories

Philip VI appealed to David to provide a diversion and hopefully force the English to re-deploy troops along their own northern border.

David was more than willing to oblige. In the autumn of that fateful year a Scottish host marched south, swinging through Cumberland to ravage the north. Lanercost was sacked, as was the priory at Hexham, though the town was left intact to serve as a rearward supply base. In October the Scots plunged across the rivers Tyne and Derwent, plundering their way to Durham via Ebchester. By the 16th their host was encamped within sight of the city at 'Beau Repaire', (Bearpark).

Meanwhile, the English had not been idle. As the King would not be diverted from his conquests in France the northern lords resolved to meet the Scottish threat themselves. Under the banner of the Archbishop of York the northerners mustered at Auckland, some 19 miles distant from their foes. On the 17th the English, perhaps numbering as many as 15,000, felt strong enough to advance from their base toward Herrington and from there to Ferry-on-the-Hill. The intention being to shadow any further Scots advance and gauge the strength of their forces.

At this juncture it seems obvious that the Scots had allowed their easy passage to lull them into a false sense of security, effectively surrendering the initiative.

Certainly their intelligence seems lacking, the first hint they received was when a raiding party under Sir William Douglas ran into the English vanguard. This negligence cost them dear, the impetuous Scots were routed and pursued to within sight of their main body, leaving a bloody trail of casualties.

Having thus tested the mettle of the English, Douglas advised the King to withdraw and avoid battle, even though the Scots enjoyed numerical superiority, perhaps by as many as 5,000 men. The King would not brook such a loss of face and resolved upon an immediate attack, not as it transpired, a particularly wise decision.

By now the English were deploying along a shallow ridge running north to south almost within bowshot of Bearpark. The position was marked by an ancient cross, one of a series ringing Durham, this one being Neville's Cross. Appropriately enough, the army was led by Ralph Neville, whose conduct during the coming battle would earn him the right to be buried in Durham Cathedral — the first layman to be accorded such an honour. The English enjoyed a favourable vantage, their flanks protected, on the right, by the rivers Dearness and Broughton, and on the left by the City itself and the Wear. The ridge rose by no more than 200 ft. but provided the English archers with an excellent field of fire.

Their army was drawn up in three main divisions, Henry Percy

Typical English longbow in use throughout the period of the Scottish Wars, as developed from the Welsh longbow first encountered by Edward I during his campaigns in Wales.

67

commanded the right, with Neville in the centre and Sir Thomas
Rokeby on the left. The Archbishop and his court were placed behind
Rokeby's division — on a hill known as Maidens Bower the prior of
Durham and his monks bore the holy cloth, (the corporal or corporax
which St. Cuthbert used to cover the chalice in the eucharist service).
God, on this day, was surely an Englishman. Of greater military
significance was the cavalry reserve, commanded by Edward Balliol,
whose position, in a fold amongst the undulating Red Hills was
obscured from the Scots.

The invading host was also split into three, Douglas commanded the
right, the King the centre, and Robert, the High Steward, the left. The
broken ground before the ridge impeded the Scottish advance and
prevented them from forming a united front, worse, a sharp ravine
cutting Crossgate Moor baulked Douglas' line of attack. Pushed to the
left by this natural obstacle his men began to crowd the royal troops in
the centre, further slowing the pace of the onslaught.

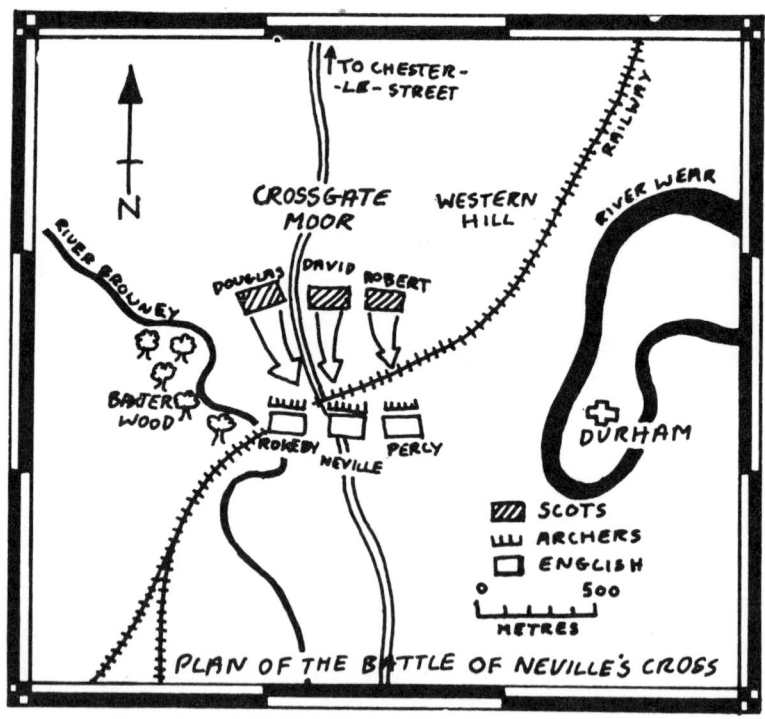

PLAN OF THE BATTLE OF NEVILLE'S CROSS

As at Halidon the Scots had now presented a perfect target for the
longbowmen, grouped in front of each of the English divisions.
Bowstrings thrummed and Scots began to fall, in their haste they had
forgotten the lessons that the former carnage should have taught. It
was the High Steward's division who charged through the clothyard

storm, to scatter the English archers and, by dint of their furious attack, push back the leading ranks. This advantage was lost when Balliol threw his cavalry reserve into a series of lightning flank attacks, never allowing his men to scatter and plunder, as was their natural bent, but keeping the pressure on the Scots whose offensive now gave way to the defensive. Hampered by the unfavourable ground and assailed by the English horse, the Scottish flank divisions began to give ground. With mounting casualties and an increasingly untenable position they faced defeat in detail. As the English kept up the pressure the Scottish host began to break up, both flanks dissolving in rout. For a while the centre struggled beneath the royal banner but, virtually surrounded, were forced to give ground and desperate resistance soon give way to flight.

Crossgate Moor became a boiling torrent of desperate survivors, harried and hacked down by the victorious English, exacting full recompense for the injuries they had earlier sustained. Exhausted and wounded King David sought a hiding place beneath the span of Aldin Grange Bridge where he was captured by a Northumbrian Knight, John Copeland. The heaps of Scottish slain on Crossgate Moor bore mute testimony to the fact that the invasion of 1346 was over.

All in all it had been a very good year for the English. David II, defeated and humiliated, was conveyed to the Tower, his ill fated attempt to ease the pressure on his allies had achieved nothing beyond adding another victory to the English roll.

The site of the battle is today largely obscured by subsequent development, though the line of the present railway crosses the ridge and roughly shows the English position. The southward course of the A167 follows the line along which Douglas may have advanced, the ravine out by the River Browney and, which caused such confusion to the Scots, can still be traced.

Yeavering, 1415.

Englishman and Scot clashed again at Yeavering in the same year that King Harry's longbowmen decimated the French host at Agincourt.

Long before the days of chivalry, the summit of that domed knoll known as Yeavering Bell had been crowned by an Iron Age fort whose stone ramparts gird the hill.

Beneath the crowding heights, on the flat plain by the river, King Edwin built his fine palace of Gefrin. Close to the presumed site of Edwin's palace, itself commemorated by a large roadside marker, stands a stone memorial erected in memory of the English triumph. Here, secured by the subtle influences of the Christianised prince,

Paulinus, stayed, preached, converted and baptised, the first herald of that new and Golden Age that Christianity would help bring to Northumbria.

It was later, much later, long after the Golden Age had slipped into history that the border skirmish, known as the battle of Getereyne occurred, fought on Magdalen Day, (22nd July), 1415.

A large body of Scots, said to be four thousand strong, had slipped over the border and harried unopposed until, at Yeavering, they were met by a flying column led by the Earl of Westmorland and Robert Umfraville, a doughty fighter known as 'Robin-mend-the-market'.

The English numbered no more than 'Seven-score spearmen' and three hundred bowmen. Nevertheless, the suddenness and vigour of the attack thoroughly rattled the marauders who were utterly routed and fled back into Scotland, jubilantly harassed by the victorious English who carried on the pursuit for a good twelve miles. Behind them the Scots left sixty dead and three hundred more as captive.

This was scarcely a major encounter, though it did much to boost the reputations of the English commanders — Umfraville later sailed to France with the English army toward a still more resounding triumph.

The site, so far as it can be traced, lies adjacent to the B6351, five or six miles N.W. of Wooler, beneath the fortress clad summit of Yeavering Bell.

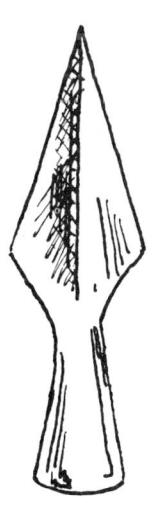

Lance-heads
14th-15th
Century.

Chapter Three

DOUGLAS AND PERCY

It fell about the Lammas tide,
When the muir men win their hay,
The doughty Douglas bound him to ride
Into England, to drive a prey.

Ballad of Chevy Chase

Fewer rivalries have attracted greater attention or inspired more epic balladry than the enmity between Douglas and Percy that at once embodies the folly, brutality, courage and glory of knighthood. The power of both families at least rivalled, and sometimes nearly surpassed, that of their respective rulers. Both were schooled in a martial tradition. Hotspur and the Douglas were the greatest paladins of their age, the Hector and Achilles of their day, men in whom honour and courage, vanity and cruelty were inextricably mixed. They have inspired generations of poets and writers and yet they themselves destroyed far more than they created, lived by and for the sword and usually perished by it. The cause for which they rode was seldom more glorious than naked brigandry, and yet their fame has endured as figures only marginally less romantic than their dim predecessors at King Arthur's court.

Horseman's axe
c. 1400.

The Douglas clan are a family of ancient lineage and were for long a power to be reckoned with on the Scottish side of the border. It appears that the first recorded chief of the clan was Sir William de Douglas, who witnessed a charter between 1114 and 1199. It was his grandson, another William, known as Sir 'Hardi' who sired the legendary Jamie Douglas — 'Black Douglas' who was Bruce's formidable friend and ally throughout the long struggle against the English invaders. He perished, with typical bravado, in an insignificant skirmish against the Moors in Spain in 1330 whilst engaged upon his final mission for his old friend and leader, carrying that hero's heart to the Holy Land in a silver casket.

This almost quixotic flirtation with violent death runs like a thread through the Douglas history, for they were ever a warlike clan, and those chieftains who survived long enough to die in their beds were a distinct minority. Many was the Scottish host that mustered beneath the Douglas banner and followed that standard to death or victory. The

72

former eventuality, unfortunately, was not uncommon and though none could ever question their often reckless valour their tactical wisdom was sometimes less apparent. Archibald Douglas led a Scottish army to bloody ruin at Halidon Hill and perished himself in the carnage.

His son, yet another William, was created Earl of Douglas and then later, through an advantageous marriage, secured the earldom of Mar. Following his remarkably peaceful demise in 1381 he was succeeded by his son James who, reverting more to type, led a Scottish force to posthumous glory upon the field of Otterburn a mere seven years later.

A Douglas, aptly named the 'Tineman' or 'loser' led a Scottish force to destruction at Homildon whilst the fourth earl who was created Duke of Touraine in 1424, fell in battle at Verneuil the very same year. The sixth earl died by the axe at Edinburgh in 1440, but his successor was created first Earl of Avondale and, even more remarkable, lasted long enough to be among that scarce band of those who expired from purely natural causes. Continuing in the true tradition, however, his half dozen sons plunged madly into the mêlée of Scottish politics and wars, usually synonymous. One fell, unsuspecting, to the assassin's dagger at the court of his jealous monarch, James II, at Stirling in 1452, a second died at the battle of Arkinholm, a third being summarily executed after that affray. A fourth son went to the block in 1463.

As appears more than obvious the Douglases were no strangers to war and bloodshed, in the house of Percy they would find an adversary as equally dedicated to the arts of war, as equally noble in lineage, and with the same propensity for careless gallantry.

William de Percy was a Norman knight who crossed the channel in the wake of the victory at Hastings as a follower of Hugh D'Avranches, the conqueror's nephew. Even then, the Percies could trace an honourable descent that dated back to the dark days of the Norse inroads and a roving chieftain named Manifred who finally settled, sometime during the ninth century, in the village of Percy from whence his descendants derived their patronym.

William had been allotted some estates in Yorkshire and cemented his good fortune by marrying the Saxon heiress whose father had fallen in the fight against the very invaders who now settled so easily upon his lands. Even during these earlier years the Percies were oft seduced by the scent of war and their banner fluttered alongside those of the saints at the Battle of the Standard, later they joined in the barons revolt against King John.

The 19th November, 1309, was a significant date in the history of the county of Northumberland for it was on that day that the Percies purchased the Barony of Alnwick from Bek, Bishop of Durham and thus began their long association with the area. Thereafter the history of Percy and of Northumberland is almost one and the same. So many of the clan bore the Christian name of Henry that it is common for them to be numbered as for royalty. It was the third of that name who had bought Alnwick, thus becoming the 1st Earl Percy of Alnwick and it was he who began expanding the modest fort into the castellated residence, suitable for one of his rank and standing. When finally completed the Percy stronghold could contain a garrison force of over three thousand and ranked as one of the most formidable holds throughout the border marches, no mean boast in a land that was scarcely lacking in fortifications.

The first Earl did not confine his martial activities solely to the realm of military architecture, but found time to pursue the more lethal diversions of actual campaigning and he suffered in the humiliating rout of the English chivalry at Bannockburn. This debacle bred scant affection for the monarch, Edward II and the Earl conspired vigorously against the royal favourite Piers Gaveston and his own successor, the fourth Henry, was active in the overthrow of Edward

Warkworth, Shakespeare's 'worm-eaten hold of ragged stone'. (Henry IV pt II — prologue.)

himself. With the restraining influence of the king removed Percy assumed the role of Warden of the Marches, adding Warkworth to his holdings. This same Earl fought at the protracted siege of Berwick, shared in the carnage of Halidon Hill, and later clashed yet again with

the Scots at Neville's Cross. Not to be outshone by his vigorous father, the son meanwhile stood beneath King Edward's standard at Crecy.

The fourth Earl enjoyed the patronage of Richard II who created him first Earl of Northumberland and then later, Earl Marshall of England. In spite of such bounty the Earl did not feel constrained by any ties of loyalty to the monarch against whom he actively plotted, welcoming the usurper Bolingbroke. It was this Earl's eldest son, yet again, named Henry, though better known to history as 'Hotspur' who would rank above all his kin as a doughty fighter. The nickname was earned at an early age from the Scots, his first enemy, but from the time of his knighthood at the coronation of Richard II to the day of his bloody demise at Shrewsbury Hotspur's sword seldom rested in its scabbard.

He was, for a time, Governor of Berwick and also later of Calais, at a time when a major French offensive seemed in the offing. He was elected knight of the Garter and the English armies that sought out the rebel Glendower were under his command. It was during the course of the latter campaign that Hotspur spent vast sums from his own amply stocked coffers to support the royal army in Wales. This expenditure, for which he was not reimbursed, formed the initial basis of the rift between the Percies and the King.

Throughout his career Hotspur was the doyen of medieval chivalry, the beau sabreur of the age, an image later immortalised by the bard himself. It was, ironically, his dramatic victory at Homildon that ultimately led to his downfall. The king's conduct in demanding both the custody of and the ransom from the prisoners that proved to be the final straw in the impending row, which, when it erupted, led straight onto the road to rebellion and the bloody day at Shrewsbury, where even the combined talents of Douglas and Percy failed to prevail.

Cannily, Northumberland himself was absent from the field of slaughter 'Crafty sick', as Shakespeare would have us believe, and thereafter he patched up a sham reconciliation with the king. Needless to add, he continued to conspire against him as heartily as ever until a final uprising in 1409 that culminated in the batle of Bramham Moor, when the old fox was finally brought to ground and devoured by the hounds.

Northumberland was shortly followed to the grave by Henry IV himself and after his death the king, Henry V, Shakespeare's 'Prince Hal' graciously reinstated the Percies to their sequestered estates. He restored Algernon, Hotspur's son, to his grandfathers's title, thus nobly discharging the debt he seems to have felt toward his old mentor from the Welsh campaigns.

Profiting from the sanguinary experiences of his predecessors the

Henry Percy —
'Hotspur'.

new Earl contrived to die peacefully in his bed, but by the middle of the fifteenth century the nation as a whole was plunged into the bloody turmoil of internecine strife as followers of the red and white roses struggled bitterly and savagely for supremacy. Predictably the Percies dashed headlong into the midst of the carnage:

> . . . Whereat the great lord of Northumberland,
> Whose warlike ears could never brook retreat,
> Cheer'd up the drooping army; and himself
> Lord Clifford and Lord Stafford, all a-breast,
> Charged our main battle's front, and breaking in
> Were by the swords of common soldiers slain . . .
>
> (III Henry VI, 1:1).

Thus, a Percy Earl fell at St. Albans in 1455. Four of his sons then followed him, sword in hand, to the grave, including the succeeding Earl who died at Towton (1461), and Sir Ralph Percy slain upon the field of Hedgeley Moor in 1464.

Even when the last alarums had faded away and the dust settled over Bosworth field, yet another Earl died violently in the service of Henry VII. His, however, was no glorious end upon the battlefield, but a sordid death at the hands of a mob from whom he was trying to extract taxation on behalf of the new ruler. It is ironic that this Earl should have died for the cause of cashflow rather than glory, but it is perhaps in keeping with the mercantile spirit of the dawning Renaissance. Nevertheless the history of the borders was to resound to the clash between Douglas and Percy, a clash that was consecrated in the blood of their followers and immortalised in legend and ballad.

Otterburn, 19th August, 1388, NT880940.

> The Percy and the Douglas mette:
> That ether of other was fayne;
> They struck together,
> With swords of fyne Cologne.
>
> Tyll the bloode from ther helmets ranne,
> As the mist doth in the rayne
> Yelde the to me sayd the Douglas
> Our ells thour schalt be slayne.

77

[1]The fact that Otterburn has so long been celebrated in song and verse indicates just how bloody an encounter it must have been, and in an era when bloody encounter was far from rare.

The battle came in the wake of the widespread political uncertainty and instability during the reign of Richard II. The unhappy tribulations of that ill-fated monarch seemed to provide an ideal opportunity for a large scale incursion from north of the border. Needless to say, such opportunities did not go unnoticed, and the 'auld enemie' prepared to pounce.

Wasting little time in preparation, a Scots army was swiftly assembled, and gathered at Jedburgh. By 5th August the invasion force was ready and the leaders repaired to the isolated church at Southdean[2] to make final preparation.

The Scots planning was meticulous, less so their security, for an English spy was able to penetrate their counsels and glean details of the plan. On attempting to make good his escape, however, the agent discovered, and we can imagine his dismay, that his horse had been stolen. Such dishonest borrowing was very much a border custom but the horse thief cannot have imagined the service which, albeit unwittingly, he was performing for his country. One who has the appearance of a gentleman and yet seemingly prefers to travel on foot, would always attract attention from suspicious sentinels. It was not long until the Englishman, unable to withstand the lesser subtleties of medieval interrogation, had blurted out the welcome awaiting the invaders. It transpired that the English did not yet feel strong enough in numbers to meet the Scots in open battle. They therefore planned to let the invaders cross the border unopposed and then, they themselves, would sweep into Scotland and create such havoc as would leave the Scots no option but to come pelting back. This manoeuvre would buy enough time to raise sufficient troops to provide a fuller welcome for any future incursion. For the English, the most pressing question was whether the Scots planned to attack down the east, or the west coast.

To add to the confusion the Scots resolved upon a double-pronged attack. The bulk of the invaders, led by the Earl of Fife, would launch their offensive in the west, whilst a smaller diversionary force swept down the east coast.

This latter body would be commanded by the Earls of Douglas, March and Moray. James, Earl of Douglas, crossed the Tweed with his

---

[1]   'The Battle of Otterbourne'
      Reliques of Ancient Poetry Bishop Piercy.

[2]   The remains of this church can still be seen and a plaque at the site commemorates the campaign.
      Bonchester Bridge NT 632092 1765.

fellow Earls, three thousand spearmen and two thousand men-at-arms.

This was no casual raiding party but a drilled and disciplined body of troops. The armoured infantrymen had all benefited from a recent consignment of arms originating from France; glad as always of any opportunity of striking a blow against the perfidious English. The spearmen, whose ancestors had smashed King Edward's feudal host at Bannockburn, marched solidly beneath the burden of the cumbersome eighteen foot pike. Gentlemen, Knights, and Lords rode like odd patches of gaudy flashing colour amid the dull leather clad ranks, the sun glinting off polished plate and burnished mail. The invaders swept through the county of Northumberland, their passing marked as always by burning thatch and widow's keening. Once into Durham the Douglas paused to give full vent to his army's considerable talent for destruction. As the Scots slaughtered and pillaged in the Durham countryside the narrow streets of the city seethed with the horde of refugees crammed behind the defences. Every night the summer skies would glow with the light of burning hamlets, the overpowering mass of the great cathedral a solitary outpost of peace, beset by the dogs of war. An English army was swiftly mustered in North Yorkshire but remained on the defensive, awaiting the Scots continued advance. The ruse had worked, and brilliantly. As the defenders waited inert, Douglas swiftly recalled his scattered battalions, herded his men into a line of march and began to fall back. It was only as the Scottish column recrossed the Tyne that the English commanders awoke to the deception, though, by them, it seemed too late.

The Earl of Northumberland had, all the while, remained barricaded at Alnwick, professing an intention to check the Scots eventual withdrawal. His two sons, Sir Henry (Hotspur), and Sir Ralph were despatched to Newcastle to bolster the thin ranks of defenders. There were some minor alarms and excursions as the retreating invaders passed the city though they had neither the time nor the means to mount a full scale attack. Legend insists that Hotspur and Douglas met in single combat before the walls of Newcastle. The upshot of the encounter was that Douglas made off with the Percy's bannaret, a considerable loss of face for a knight of such touchy honour. We hear that the Douglas offered to delay his retreat in order to provide his spirited opponent with an opportunity for a return bout, and a chance to regain his lost colours. Such gallantry has considerable romantic appeal, but scant foundation in reality. By now the Scots army was heavy laden with booty and the slow ox-drawn, waggons and carts, piled high with their ill gotten loot, would slow the army down dramatically.

Douglas led his forces, at an enforced, leisurely pace, northward through Ponteland where the castle was stormed and slighted, arriving eventually at Otterburn. Here the castle proved a tougher nut altogether and all attempts at an escalade were repulsed. Lacking any proper siege train Douglas was obliged to abandon the attack, withdrawing to his camp which was about one thousand metres north of the Rede, adjacent to some ancient earthworks[1].

Hotspur, smarting from his earlier humiliation, was determined that the Scots should not escape unscathed. Whilst Ponteland smouldered, an English force was being mustered and following a forced march from Newcastle reached Otterburn on the evening of the 19th August — St. Oswin's eve.

At first, Hotspur was unaware of the proximity of this quarry, as the Scots camp was screened by a stand of timber. Despite the fact he was leading a scratchbuilt army that had just covered thirty miles by forced march, Hotspur, with characteristic elan and recklessness, resolved upon an immediate night attack. The plan involved a double pronged attack, consisting of the Umfraville[2] contingent which was to circle around and take the Scots in the rear and a frontal assault led by Hotspur himself. In view of the darkness and the uncertainty of the Scottish position, which there had not been time to reconnoitre, these manoeuvres were likely to prove extremely hazardous and uncertain.

First to come unstuck was Hotspur himself, who advancing pell mell upon the supposed enemy position, mistook a waggon park for the main camp. Though few, the Scottish defenders put up a stiff fight, alerting the Douglas to his peril and giving their comrades time to prepare. By now the Umfravilles had also come to grief, their night march and faulty navigation led them too far north. Consequently, they were in no position to hinder the Scots as Douglas drove a furious counterattack against the right of Hotspur's vanguard.

As the mass of English and Scots finally came to grips an eerie combat ensued. Clouds, scudding across the face of the moon, at first obscured, and then threw the ghastly scene in strange relief like glimpses of some Dantesque nightmare. The recurrent darkness shut out the sights, but not the sounds, of slaughter. Injured and dying screamed and thrashed in the tussocky grass, the bodies of the dead strewn, sacklike, amongst the carnage. The noise was everywhere,

---

[1]   Probably this camp was on Fawdon Hill ¾ mile N.E. of Otterburn or perhaps the old British camp N.W. of Holt Wood above Greenchesters.

[2]   Led by Sir Thomas Umfraville, the Umfravilles were lords of Redesdale and Prudhoe, though the latter had passed to the Percies by marriage in 1375. Thomas was the bastard son of another Sir Thomas who held Harbottle, Holmside and Otterburn.

deafening, the din of steel against steel, rasping from plate and mail, battering wooden targets, cleaving through helmet and skull; archers, their weapon's twanging, as deadly missiles sought their shadowy targets. Hotspur's bold attack had led him into trouble; unsupported by his other contingent, still stumbling around the country on their nocturnal peregrination, he was faced with the full fury of the Scots onslaught and it began to look as though the Douglas might score another victory.

> His host he parted had in 3,
> As leader ware and try'd,
> And soon his spearmen on their foes
> Bare down on every side.
>
> Throughout the English Archery,
> They dealt fill many a wound:
> But still our valiant Englishmen
> All firmly kept their ground.

Another break in the clouds showed Hotspur the hated Douglas standard waving proudly in the breeze and he hurled his tired men forward again, determined to close with the Scottish commander. Fighting around the standard was fierce and merciless, Sir Patrick Hepburn and his two sons fell in its defence. The wandering Umfravilles at last had managed to locate the Scots camp, by now, of course, deserted. Stolidly they pushed on, drawn by the noise of the battle, eventually regaining their comrades on the right flank. Fresh, and unblooded, they thrust into the fray; the renewed impetus threatened to break the Scots line, and the Douglas must have sensed that defeat was just around the corner.

In a lone, desperate bid to turn the fatal tide Douglas hurled himself upon the English line, battle axe cleaving a bloody swathe through the tightly packed ranks. With a few brave followers, the Scottish leader hacked his way through the opposing mass, cutting down all who came against him. Finally he fell, bleeding from wounds to the head and body, the blood pumping freely from a great gash in the thigh. His standard bearer and Sir John Hart lay dead beside him, only his chaplain, William of North Berwick, who had temporarily abandoned the cloth for the broadsword, survived. Alone, this redoubtable churchman held off the press of English closing in upon the dying Earl. Presently Sir James Lindsay with Sir John and Sir Walter Sinclair came up and the English fell back. Knowing that his death was near, Douglas, with admirable élan, reminded his dismayed followers that

Sword c. 1380.

81

few of his line ever died in their beds, and as long as the standard was kept aloft and the famous slogan 'A Douglas, A Douglas' repeated, all was not lost.

Though he presently expired, few on either side were aware of the Earl's demise and the fight continued with fury unabated. All through the long night the battle raged, and the longer it went on the more their earlier forced marching began to tell upon the English. Strength and morale ebbed before fatigue, the line began to founder and then to break. In ones and twos, then in groups and finally in droves the English fled. Hotspur and his brother Ralph, caught by the folly of their own furious valour, were prisoners. Sir Hugh Montgomery made captive an exhausted Hotspur, though Ralph, would not submit till the blood of his wounds flowed liberally from hose and greaves. Their leaders taken, the English broke completely and the inevitable rout ensued. Soon, another thousand joined their captains in captivity.

Dawn revealed a scene of dreadful carnage. Dead and captive, the English had lost nearly three thousand men. In arms and equipment the hastily mustered Northumbrians were vastly inferior to their foes who had been in the field for a month and had been amply armed and accoutred by the French. In all, the Scots lost only a few hundred, so they had much for which to thank their allies. Douglas was later interred at Melrose. Perhaps their greater experience added to the Scots morale and cohesion, certainly they had made no forced marches on the day of the battle. Darkness prevented full use of the fearsome longbow, perennial scourge of Scottish spearmen. Hotspur can be criticised for his rashness in launching so sudden, and perhaps so unconsidered an attack, but no soldier can deny the tremendous advantage of surprise so nearly gained, and yet, so dearly lost. Perhaps Hotspur, whose courage can never be questioned, may even have envied his dead rival dying the perfect hero's death like Nelson, in the very hour of his triumph. Froissart, whose chronicles cover many such engagements, had this to say about the field of Otterburn:—

'Of all the battles and encounterings that I have made mention of heretofore in all this history, great or small, this battle that I treat of now was one of the sorest and best foughten without cowardice or faint hearts'.

Today the battle field is marked by Percy's Cross, though an earlier monument, known as the battle stone, stood some one hundred and fifty yards to the east of this.

When the turnpike from Otterburn to Redesdale was built, in 1777, the Duke of Northumberland offered to build a memorial near the

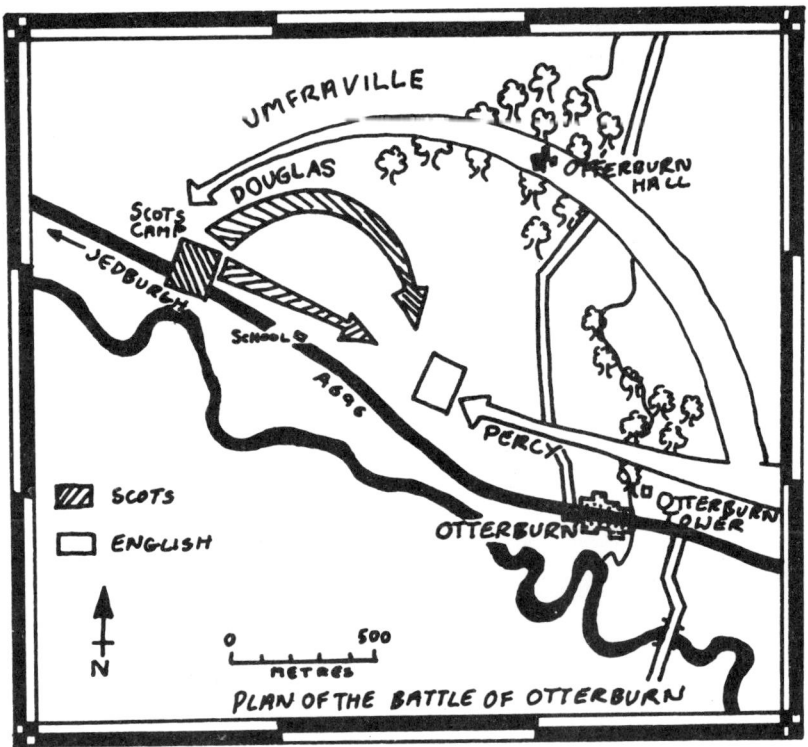

PLAN OF THE BATTLE OF OTTERBURN

road. The owner of the land a Mr. Ellison of Otterburn, felt that the Duke might use this as an excuse to claim the land for himself, so Mr. Ellison volunteered to erect the memorial instead, the result being that which we see today.

The fame of Otterburn is largely owed to the balladry it inspired, an epic and bloody clash between two such noble paladins is the very stuff of poetry and romance. A more hard-minded approach would be to view the battle simply as a pointless, bloody vendetta typical of the mindless barbarism of the period when nobles were free to enjoy their passion for blood-letting, regardless of the monumental death and suffering caused to others. Perhaps, we can leave the final judgement to the words of Sir Philip Sydney, himself the doyen of chivalry in his age, and destined also to die gloriously upon the battlefield:—

'I never heard the old song of Piercy and Douglas, that I found not my heart more moved than with a trumpet; and yet it is sung by some blind crowder with no rougher voice than rude stile; which being so evil apparelled in the dust and cobweb of that uncivil age, what would it work trimmed in the gorgeous eloquence of Pindar.'

The field of Otterburn is largely unchanged from 1388, Percy's

Percy's Cross —
Otterburn.

Cross is situated just north of Otterburn on the A696, the church at Elsdon and the Norman motte are well worth a visit.

The Battle of Homildon Hill, 1402.

> On Holyrood Day the gallant Hotspur there,
> Young Harry Percy, and brave Archibald,
> That ever valiant and approved Scots
> At Holmedon met.
>
> (I Henry IV 1:1)

Northward from Wooler, the first outriders of the Cheviots hang over the narrow glens below, arrayed, almost as a primeval bodyguard, around the massif itself. Hunched, bare, worn by the seasons of the ages, glowering down the fertile Milfield plain which, until well into the seventeenth century, remained little more than a morass, whose quaking entrails provided refuge for local reivers and outlaws.

The nearest of the hills to Wooler is Humbleton, known to history as Homildon. Here, was fought one of the greatest of all border battles.

84

Here, the impetuous Hotspur took ample revenge upon the Douglases for his defeat at Otterburn fourteen years before, but also, in the process, sowed the roots of his own violent demise at Shrewsbury, the following year.

As a textbook battle it was remarkable. A body of archers, unsupported throughout, and from an inferior position attacked, and ultimately routed, a well armed force, some times larger than themselves.

The battle followed a massive incursion, led by Archibald Douglas, once a favoured Scottish commander, whose luck is always said to have deserted him after the murder of the Duke of Rothsay, a fellow Scot. Subsequently, he earned the unenviable nickname of 'Tineman' or 'lose-man', a reputation hardly to be enhanced by the carnage to come.

Douglas's raid is supposed to have been retaliatory, following the defeat and decimation of an early band of invaders. This force had been led by one Hepburn of Hailes who fell together with many of his followers when ambushed by Douglas' sworn enemy the exiled Earl of March[1] at West Nisbet.

The army that marched into England was ten thousand strong, spearmen, men at arms, and a fine gathering of Scottish knights including the Earls of Moray, of Angus and Fergus MacDonald of Galloway. Pushing as far south as the Tyne, the Scots pillaged and slew until, heavily burdened with booty, they attempted to withdraw into Scotland.

Streaming out from the coastal fortress of Bamburgh, came a strong body of English knights and men at arms, backed by roughly one thousand archers. They were led by Hotspur, the Earl of Northumberland, and the experienced Earl of March.

The ballads tells us that these archers were men from the three shires of Bamburgh, Hexham and Norham, however, historians, who have consulted the original muster rolls, tell a different story. The victors of Homildon were Welshmen. This is less surprising, when we consider that Hotspur had lately been engaged against Owen Glendower on behalf of Henry IV. Not only were the Welshmen formidable with the longbow, but it was prudent politics to keep them occupied and away from home. The Welsh Marches had ever been loyal to the deposed Richard II, whose sudden and violent demise had not endeared their new monarch to them.

On the 13th September, with only twelve miles to go to the friendly fords along the Tweed and safety beyond, the invaders found their passage blocked by Hotspur's army approaching from the east.

[1] George Dunbar, Earl of March, a former ally of the Douglas quarrelled with him over a marriage settlement.

Scrambling up the steep, tussocky slopes of Homildon, the Scots drew up around the crest of the hill. Hotspur, as eager for glory as ever, and anxious to be in the thick of the fight, was nevertheless restrained by the wiser counsels of the Earl of March.

The English drew up at the foot of the hill, but only the force of archers moved forward. Advancing by companies, and in regular order, despite the steepness of the terrain, they commenced pouring volleys of the redoubtable 'cloth-yard' shafts into the inert, dense packed ranks of the Scots above. Even the fine plate of the Scottish nobility offered but scant protection and the lesser clad footsoldiers began falling in droves. Douglas, with his ill-fortune running true to form, amply assisted by his own ineptitude, appeared paralysed by these developments and made no attempt to regain the initiative, whilst all around his followers succumbed to the hissing, rain of death spitting from the skies, especially the unarmoured Gallowegians.

Amongst the Scots were two knights, Swinton and Gordon, between whom there was a longstanding feud. Enraged by the increasing slaughter around him the elder, Swinton, determined that he at least would not die so helplessly. Calling upon his comrades to follow he prepared to charge:

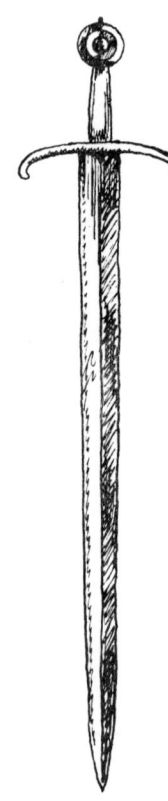

'Oh my brave countrymen what fascination had seized you that you stand to be shot at like deer instead of displaying your ancient courage and meeting your enemies hand to hand. Let those who will follow me that we may gain the victory or die'.

This impromptu battlefield oratory so impressed the more youthful Gordon that he promptly approached the other, begged that they should cease their feud and lead the attack together. Such a touching homily, beloved of Victorian romantics, at last galvanised the Scots into action, and they swarmed forward into the offensive.

Despite such a gallant beginning the charge was a stillborn thing. Disheartened and depleted, the Scots were no match for the costly, murderous fire of the archers, who steadily fell back before the onslaught, stemming the invaders belated fury with a further welter of arrows. Neither Swinton nor Gordon survived the charge.

Constantly stung by the interminable storm of missiles, the Scots attempted to descend the other flank of the hill, then to re-form and charge again on more level ground. Hotspur sensed that this was to be the moment of glory when his own knights and men at arms smashed into the thinning ranks. Again, however, the cautious counsels of the Earl of March prevailed and the bowmen were directed to carry on the fight unaided.

Sword *c.* 1420.

Still in a tight formation, the archers swerved about to meet the oncoming offensive from the lower slopes and again, the charge was halted. This last reversal snapped the tattered will of the survivors, the Scotsmen broke and ran for home. Still the bowmen had not done, casting aside their bows the lightly clad Welshmen fell upon their fleeing foes with cudgel, axe and sword.

The retreat swiftly degenerated into a total rout. Of the surviving Scots it is said that nearly five hundred drowned in the Till in their frantic efforts to gain the Tweed, and Scotland.

Behind they left another thousand dead including Sir John Livingstone, Sir Alexander Ramsey, Sir Walter Scott and Sir Walter Sinclair. Most of the surviving leaders were made captive, including Douglas himself, who had lost an eye and sustained five other wounds in the fight.

The ransom haul also included two more earls, two barons and eighty knights.

> In faith it is a conquest for a prince to boast of
> (I Henry IV 1:1)

Homildon was a resounding victory and the jubilant balladeers were swift to record:

> In blind red clouds the sun arose,
> Which saw that fatal day,
> Where breathless on the green hill side,
> Fu mony a braw Scot lay.
>
> For sair the English bowmen gall'd
> The van that ungeared stood,
> Nae thirsty shafts 'een reached the earth
> Unstained in Scottish blood.

One incident alone survives to mar the English glory. Hotspur, usually recognised as a paladin of chivalry, disgraced himself and alienated many of his own followers by what seems to have been nothing more than an act of wanton cruelty. From amongst the captives he singled out Sir William Stuart of Forest, whom he swore had been a native of England, and therefore a traitor at the time of battle. Forest was several times acquitted of this by jury, but Hotspur abused his own power to bring about the knight's execution, a course apparently motivated by nothing more than personal malice.

Stuart was consequently drawn and quartered, the remains being exposed upon the gates of York. Ironically this barbarism was soon to be repeated upon Hotspur himself, for these very prisoners proved to be his undoing and the ruin of his family.

Henry IV already owed the Percies a considerable amount, spent on his behalf in Wales. He now demanded that the captives be surrendered to him — a gross outrage upon medieval custom. This was too much for the headstrong Northumbrian, and it launched him on that short road to his sanguinary end at Shrewsbury.

> For worms brave Percy; Fare thee well great heart! —
> Ill weaved ambition, how much thom art shrunk!
> When that this body did contain a spirit,
> A kingdom for it was too small a bound!
>
> (I Henry IV v:iv)

The site is commemorated by the Bendor Stone at Red Riggs, two miles outside Wooler on the A697, there is no inscription, it is merely a very rude stone marker.

Piper Dene, 1435?, NT830350.

This little known border skirmish, fought roughly two miles south of Wark, and a mile and half west of Mindrum Hill, is a poor relation to the two preceding battles. Throughout their long leadership of the border wars men of the Douglas and Percy families led countless raids and forays back and forwards across the border. Often such incursions were contended, the fight at Piper Dene was just such an occasion. There were at least three differing accounts of the fight. The acceptable facts would appear to be that Henry Percy, Earl of Northumberland (he that was later slain at St. Albans), at that time warden of the English East Marches, led a raid against Scotland with a force totalling nearly four thousand.

At Piper Dene the would-be invaders were met by a Scottish force of some strength led by William Douglas, Earl of Angus, warden of the Middle Marches, Adam Hepburn of Hailes, Alexander Ramsay of Dalhousie and Alexander Elphinstone.

After a stiff fight, the English were utterly defeated and the battle ended in a rout. The exact losses on either side are open to debate. One account states that the English lost four hundred dead, including Clennell of Clennell and John Ogle and that a further three hundred were made prisoner. The same account claims that the Scots lost two

The figure wears
a complete plate
armour, *c.* 1415.

hundred men, including Alexander Elphinstone and two other knights of note.

Another source claims that the battle cost the English one thousand five hundred prisoners, but that few on either side were actually killed.

A third account states that John Ogle was the leader of the expedition, not the Earl, and that the purpose of the raid was actually political, in that the English were going to the aid of rebels fighting against King James.

From the general conflict of accounts it is not possible to say whether Northumberland himself was actually present, or if the raiders were intercepted before crossing the border, or upon their return. Whether the motive was actually political, or was simply a desire for loot seems equally uncertain. Casualties too are vague, though balancing the various accounts it seems that actual losses on both sides, were probably fairly light. Even the date of the battle is open to debate, the 30th September is generally agreed upon as the day, though whether it was 1435 or 1436 is disputed.

The site is not marked on the Ordnance map; perhaps this is not altogether surprising.

Chapter Four

LANCASTER AND YORK

In every shire with jacks and salads clean,
Misrule doth rise and maketh neighbours war
The weaker goes beneath, as oft as seen,
The mightiest his quarrel will prefer.

Anyone who had fought at Agincourt with Henry V would have not believed the state of affairs that soon developed after that monarch's untimely demise in 1422. His son and heir, Henry VI, was an infant of ten months and during his minority the government was left in the hands of a Regency council. As the war in France dragged on the glory of Agincourt disappeared beneath a mire of endless and expensive campaigns. This produced a war and a peace faction within the council. The latter seemed to be in the ascendant, when at the age of twenty two, the young monarch was married to Margaret of Anjou, a niece of the French Queen, as a final seal upon the truce of Tours. The price of peace, the surrender of Maine, was kept secret from the war party led by Richard, Duke of York. After four years, the secret finally came out and a howl of protest rose from the war party. Amidst this growing dissention, Henry remained, as he did for most of his life, saintly, unworldly and on his better days — half witted.

His new queen was of a different stamp, beautiful, ambitious, proud and determined. She was no friend to the equally ambitious Duke of York. For a while Henry's feeble grip upon sanity slipped completely and York, much to Margaret's chagrin, was appointed regent.

The Queen's apprehension was not without grounds, for the Duke had two clear claims to the throne. On the paternal side, he was descended from Edmund of York, the fifth son of Edward III; this meant that he was Henry's heir in the male line if the king died childless. On the maternal side, he was descended from Lionel of Clarence, the third son of Edward III, thereby inheriting the rights of Edmund of March which; the king's grandfather, Henry IV, had usurped.

Though he imprisoned Somerset, the Queen's favourite, York remained loyal to his mad monarch and when that unhappy individual was at last declared sane, he meekly returned the reins of power.

The rift was irreparable, however, and the barons began to settle their loyalties, either to the red rose of Lancaster, or the white rose of York. Civil War seemed inevitable and a clash occurred at St. Albans, where both Somerset and the Earl of Northumberland fell in the rout. Led by one of the most able Yorkist generals, the Earl of Warwick, known to history as the 'Kingmaker' the followers of the white rose won an important victory at Northampton.

The war was now joined in earnest. Spurred on by Queen Margaret who, like a tigress, championed the Lancastrian cause in the name of her infant son Edward, Prince of Wales. The King passed, like a helpless pawn, from side to side, with the swing of the pendulum. One bloody encounter followed another. The Yorkists were routed, in turn, at a second battle of St. Albans and again at Ludford. York himself, and his eldest son, Edmund, Earl of Rutland, were butchered at Wakefield and command of the Yorkist faction passed to his other son Edward, Earl of March. He inflicted a stunning defeat on the Lancastrians at Mortimers Cross and finally decided the issue with a snowstorm victory at Towton. After this final crushing defeat, the King and Queen fled northward to Scotland.

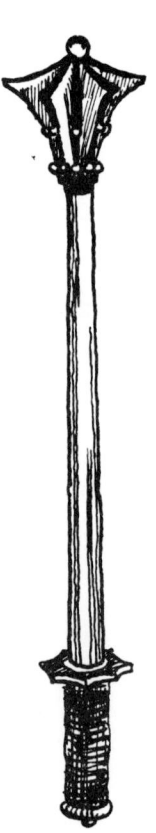

Gothic Mace
c. 1470.

With his father dead, Edward had inherited his claim to the throne, which he now usurped. Safely enthroned, as Edward IV, he delegated the campaign in the North to Warwick, undoubtedly one of the most able commanders of his day.

The feud between Lancaster and York unleashed all the fires of internecine strife upon England. The final abandonment of the French Wars in 1453, and the return to England of the knights, archers and men at arms, provided a hard core of professional soldiery ripe for mischief. Inevitably, these men drifted into the ranks of the great households, already arming for a war of their own. Their willingness and experience could only add fuel to the fire.

Once battle had been joined, the savage habits of the mercenaries exploded onto an unsuspecting population who suffered accordingly.

Northumberland was to be no exception. Inevitably the powerful Percies could not long remain aloof from the coming conflict. Though Henry Percy was restored to the earldom by Henry V, his son Thomas quarrelled with Richard Neville, Earl of Salisbury, a powerful ally of York, who naturally supported his henchman. This, inevitably, swung the Percies into the Lancastrian camp and as mentioned Thomas, Earl of Northumberland, fell at St. Albans.

The next Earl of Northumberland fell at Towton, but with the War apparently lost, the scene shifted to Northumberland, where Margaret was to lead her hapless husband into fresh misadventures.

First Battle of Hexham, 3rd April, 1463.

Edward IV sent twenty thousand men with his trusted Earl of Warwick to deal with the troublesome queen. Newcastle was besieged, and also Wark, where the fugitive Lancastrians were hiding, Lancastrian forces successfully attempted to raise the siege of Wark. This success was offset by the defection of Sir Ralph Percy, constable of Dunstanburgh, and previously a loyal Lancastrian. Margaret attempted to wrest the valuable hold of Dunstanburgh back by force, but failed miserably.

Alnwick, held by William Taillebois also capitulated and the turncoat Sir Ralph was made warden thereof. With Bamburgh also in the Yorkist grip under Sir William Tunstal, the position in Northumberland looked precarious and the royal pair were again forced to seek refuge in flight.

A year later, on October 25th, 1462, Margaret once again landed on the Northumbrian coast. Bamburgh at this time, was held by Sir Ralph Percy who, true to form, promptly changed sides again and declared for Lancaster.

In response to this new threat Warwick hurried north again and set up his H.Q. at Warkworth. As always, the Kingmaker proved a formidable opponent and by December 10th he had invested Alnwick, Dunstanburgh and Bamburgh. Presently resistance began to crumble and the fortresses surrendered. It had generally been a fairly bloodless campaign, by the standards of the day, and all of the captured garrisons were spared.

In 1463, Margaret was back again with French and Scottish forces in support. Duns was seized and then, once again, Bamburgh, again with the connivance of Sir Ralph Percy, ending that gentleman's second spell as a Yorkist. With a foothold on the coast established, Margaret now pushed inland toward Hexham, where a Yorkist force was known to be gathered.

It is likely that the Yorkists were arrayed on the right bank of Devils Water two and a half miles south east of Hexham at a spot known as 'Rel' or 'Ryal'. With typical impetuosity, Margaret threw her forces into the attack. The Yorkists, however, had a strong position and fought back stubbornly. The stiff resistance appears to have panicked Margaret's Frenchmen, who broke and fled. The panic, as ever, was contagious and the rest of the Lancastrians were soon in full flight, Hexham was to be an unlucky place for the House of Lancaster.

There is an enduring legend concerning this first battle of Hexham. It appears that in the headlong rout, the Queen and her young son, the ill-fated Prince of Wales were separated from their surviving

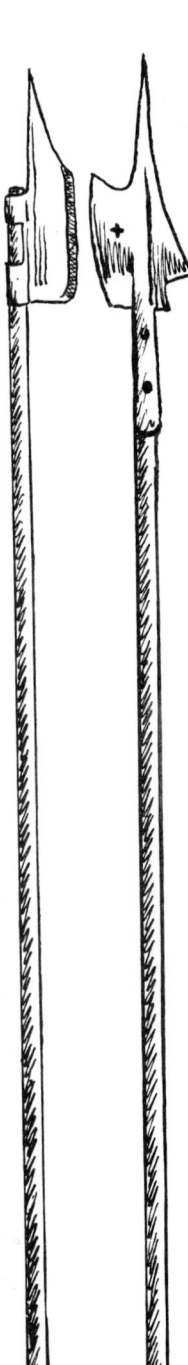

supporters and driven to seek concealment in the dense woodland adjacent to the battlefield.

Unfortunately, the woods were a nest of thieves and outlaws. The royal pair were promptly seized by a band of such villains who were content simply to rob them, unaware of the true value of their catch. Taken by the outlaws to their camp, deep in the woods, both Margaret and the prince escaped during the night to spend several days of fruitless wandering in the dense woodland, only at the end of it to be accosted by yet another outlaw.

This lone bandit, however, proved susceptible to the Queen's regal charm and bearing. He was so impressed as to declare undying fealty and, after sheltering them for several days in his own rude hideaway, conducted the royal pair safely to the coast.

There is still a cave known as the 'Queen's Cave' where this refuge is said to have been. A simple column of masonry, that roughly divides the interior, is said to have marked a tactful division of apartments. Nearby, a stretch of water is named the 'Queen Letch', supposedly being the spot where her horse stumbled and fell after the rout, thus precipitating the intriguing, if somewhat unlikely, sylvan interlude.

After the Hexham disaster, Margaret fled to Scotland to join her docile husband, persuading the Scottish king, James III to enter England and besiege Norham. With almost contemptuous ease the castle was relieved and the Scots sent scurrying northward. After this, no more than token effort, James felt free to abandon his Lancastrian charges, whose generally low success rate was making them something of a liability. After another spell in hiding the King and Queen emerged at Bamburgh, their only hold remaining. For a short period Henry VI held court in the coastal fortress, its own grey walls the total extent of his kingdom.

The situation appears too farcical even to have troubled the Yorkists who returned south, leaving Henry in splendid isolation on the Northumbrian coast.

Bowing at last to reality, the Lancastrian court deserted their shrunken domain and took sail for Flanders. The campaigning of 1463 was over, but Margaret was determined that the war should continue and that the head of the usurper, who had supplanted her feeble husband and disinherited her beloved son, should join his father on a spike astride some city gate.

The battle site is not particularly commemorated today and it is difficult for the visitor to gain a distinct impression.

Halberds *c.* 1470.

Man-at-arms mid
15th Century.

Hedgeley Moor, 25th April, 1464 (7 miles S.E. Wooler).

1464 dawned bright with apparent promise for the House of Lancaster. In England, Somerset felt confident enough to promise that the Welsh Marches and the west country were ready to rise against the House of York.

As a counter to this possible threat Warwick had induced Kennedy, the Scottish regent, to talk of peace and remove the festering sore of trouble on the northern border.

Commissioners were duly appointed from both sides and Edward's Parliament summoned at York, where terms would be discussed. The progress of the peace was soon threatened by a flurry of Lancastrian activity and an early offensive secured several strongholds in northern England, including Norham and Skipton in North Yorkshire.

The parliament was due to assemble on May 5th and it was obviously necessary to provide a strong escort for the Scots commissioners. Consequently, Lord Montagu was despatched to Northumberland with all the troops at his disposal. Somerset tried to ambush Montagu near Newcastle and, as he only had a small force at his disposal 'four score spears and bows too', he evaded the initial encounter and

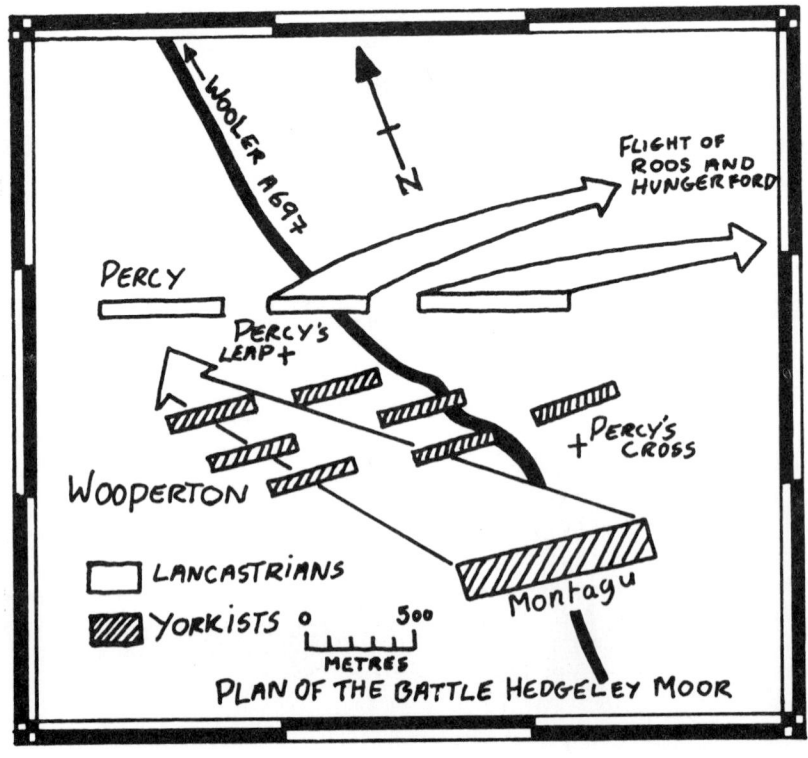

PLAN OF THE BATTLE HEDGELEY MOOR

continued northward gathering troops along the road. By the time a confrontation was finally reached at Hedgeley, his forces had grown considerably. Ranged against him were five thousand Lancastrians, led by Sir Ralph Percy, Sir Ralph Grey, Lords Hungerford and Roos. Before the battle Percy was warned that he would not survive, and that his death would be caused by the desertion of Hungerford and Roos. Ironically, this was what actually occurred. The two lords fled at the first onset and the turncoat Percy fell at last, fighting, for a cause he had so often deserted.

As he expired Percy is said to have uttered that, 'I have saved the bird in my bosom'. The exact interpretation of these enigmatic last words has never been ascertained. Inevitably, the fight now finished in a rout, with a complete Yorkist victory.

The defeat and dispersal of the Lancastrian forces enabled the Scots commissioners to proceed peacefully to York, and there conclude their peace with Edward.

On Hedgeley Moor itself, two prehistoric monoliths mark the distance known as 'Percy's Leap', apparently cleared by the dying Lancastrian in one colossal bound (a distance of some twelve yards) after receiving his death wound. A square stone shaft set up on a

Percy's Cross at Hedgeley.

97

rounded base, known as 'Percy's Cross', and bearing the Percy Arms stands some distance to the south as a memorial to the battle.

Hedgeley is just north of Glanton on the A697 and is commemorated by the cross, which stands in a farmyard.

2nd Battle of Hexham, 5th May 1464.

After the disaster at Hedgeley the surviving Lancastrians, under Somerset, retreated to Hexham where, on the levels, their unhappy monarch, Henry VI, was encamped in command, at least nominally so, of a motley host of English, French and Scots. The two important castles of Langley and Bywell were also under his domination.

Lord Montagu, however, flushed by his recent triumph at Hedgeley turned aside from his escort duty at Newcastle, from whence, in any event the Scots commissioners road to York was safe. He now marched westwards, up the Tyne Valley, with Willoughby, Greystone and four thousand men.

Warned of his approach, the Lancastrians determined to oppose his crossing of the Devils Water. This was almost a reversal of the first clash near Hexham the previous year. Now the Lancastrians were arrayed at the Linnels, some three miles east of Hexham, waiting for the attack.

Henry, displaying equal prowess as a general as he had as a King, fled westward on hearing of the Yorkist advance, leaving Somerset to command. Such an inspiring example could hardly serve to raise morale and, as the Lancastrians suffered under the further disadvantage of having the stream behind them, instead of in front, where it might at least impede the enemies advance, their overall position was not a happy one.

Meanwhile the Yorkists advanced along the north bank of the Tyne apparently unopposed, crossed the river at either Corbridge or Bywell and swept into an immediate, but well executed, attack.

As in both the previous encounters faint heartedness among the Lancastrians soon decided the day. This time it was Sir Ralph Grey who broke first, but inevitably the majority soon followed. Somerset alone, with no more than five hundred men, was left to fight it out in a hopeless rearguard action, that ended with the destruction of his force and his own capture on a hill one mile outside Hexham. The very next day he was beheaded in the town.

Lords Hungerford and Roos were discovered skulking in woods nearby and they, with Lord Taillebois, who had been found hiding in a

Glaive or Bill
c. 1470.

pit, were taken back to Newcastle for their own execution. It was said of Taillebois that:

He hadde moch mony with hym, both golde and
sylvyr that shulde hav gone unto King Harry;
and yf it had come to Harry, lat Kynge of Ingelande,
hyt wolde have causyd muche sore sorowe, for
ordynyd harneys and ordenance I nowe, but the
men wolde not go one tote wiln hym tylle they had mony.

The King's flight from Bywell, following news of the impending Yorkist advance, had been so hurried that his helmet 'Cum corona et gladius' was found there by his enemies.

Henry meanwhile, had scattered back to Bamburgh whence Sir Ralph Grey, the architect of defeat at Hexham, was also come. Again the coastal fortresses were under siege, and Dunstanburgh fell to Montagu, whose victories gained him the Earldom of Northumberland. Henry's refuge at Bamburgh was soon under attack again, and once more, the helpless monarch had to resort to flight. This time southward to Yorkshire where, in July, near Clitheroe, he was at last captured. In Northumberland, Alnwick was next to fall. The

Dunstanburgh, whose shattered walls still bear scars of bombardment.

99

encirclement of Bamburgh was complete and the castle fell by storm —
Sir Ralph Grey being taken and summarily executed.

The war in Northumberland was over. Three major encounters had
taken place and all had ended in defeat for the Lancastrians. The
eclipse of Lancaster was now complete, the second battle at Hexham
ended any last hope of victory — Somerset, Percy and Grey were dead.

None of the battles took place on a particularly large scale and
casualties, generally, were not heavy, but the second fight at Hexham
marked the virtual end of that phase of the Wars of the Roses and so
merits national, as well as local, significance.

Chapter Five

FLODDEN FIELD

Flodden, 1513.

> Green Flodden! On thy blood stain'd head
> Descend no rain nor vernal dew;
> But still, thou charnel of the dead,
> May whitening bones thy surface strew!
> Soon as I tread thy rush-clad vale,
> Wild fancy fells the clasping mail;
> The rancour of a thousand years
> Glows in my breast; again I burn
> To see banner'd pomp of war return,
> And mark, beneath the moon, the silverlight of spears!
>
> But distant fleets each warrior ghost,
> With surly sounds that murmur far;
> Such sounds were hear when Syria's host
> Roll'd from the walls of proud Samar
> Around my solitary head
> Gleam the blue lightings of the dead;
> While murmur low the shadowy band—
> Lament no more the warriors doom!
> Blood, blood, alone, should dew the hero's tomb,
> Who falls, mid circling spears to save his native land.

J. Leyden: *Ode on visiting Flodden*

A new era was dawning. The Welshman, Henry Tudor, had finally ended the long run of the Plantagenets when the Wars of the Roses reached their bloody finale in the slaughter on Bosworth field. The Yorkist, Richard III, was slain and the House of Tudor stepped into the empty throne room. In spite of his success Henry can hardly have felt secure, not only had his immediate predecessor come to such a sanguinary end but two out of three earlier monarchs had failed to emerge, alive, from the Tower. The general atmosphere of 'open season' that had attended the protracted course of the wars had not been confined to the barons and the lower orders. People were wearied of the long feud, but the very nature of war itself was changing.

For years the formidable longbow had dominated every field upon which it had appeared and yet, though the 'cloth yard' shaft laid low many an armoured knight, the knights, as a class, had survived and continued to form the backbone of feudal armies.

Around 1249 however, an Englishman, one Friar Bacon, had by the mixture of sulphur, charcoal and saltpetre, produced gunpowder, of which he was able to say:—

'It is so terrifying that whole armies may
be harmed or scattered by it.'

The full arrival of gunpowder did not take place overnight, though by 1331 a German army was using cannon in Italy.

These early cannon were scarcely sophisticated. Though smaller pieces were often cast in brass or bronze the larger guns were fashioned from staves of wrought iron, laid side by side around a timber core and then welded together. Not only was the welding a somewhat uncertain art, but there were often weak spots in the wrought iron itself. Combined with a considerable variance in the relative strengths of different sources of powder, the early gunner did not have an easy life — if for any of these reasons the gun burst on firing then he was undoubtedly a dead man. Perhaps one of the most famous persons to be slain in this fashion was James II of Scotland, who met his untimely end whilst supervising the siting of his favourite piece named 'The Lion', at the siege of Roxburgh in 1460. The King was standing by to observe the effect of his artillery upon the defences when the Lion exploded and he was killed instantly.

O' curs'd device! Base implement of death!
Framed in the black Tartarean realms beneath!
By Beelzebub's malicious art design'd
To ruin the race of human kind.

It was the unfortunate James II who is credited with the commissioning of the great gun known as 'Mons Meg', a mighty piece, with a thirteen foot length and twenty inch bore. The gun is said to have been made by one Molise McKim, the hereditary smith of Threave and the name was derived from that of his nagging wife, whose verbosity he likened to the cannon's roar.

In general these larger, heavier pieces were restricted to siege warfare where, once in position, they could be used to batter the enemies walls into oblivion. The main difficulty in the early cannon lay in transporting the unwieldy guns across difficult country and where, as on the border, this problem was acute, the effects of the cannon's development were considerably retarded. Nevertheless, the guns would still play their part at Flodden.

Though the longbow was beginning to suffer an eclipse, it still remained in widespread use. The real advantage of the early handgun was that it was very easy to operate, and did not require the constant practice at the butts.

Simply a crude iron barrel lashed to a rough batten, or stock, the handgun was fired by lighting the touchhole, in a similar fashion to larger guns. Despite their rather 'do it yourself' appearance these early handguns could inflict fearful damage upon a group of advancing enemy. Thus the great foundation of the feudal host, the innate superiority of the mounted knight, was finally swept away. A single unarmoured, untrained peasant could, by a single stroke, demolish a substantial group of his social superiors. The finest armour, the surest mount, the keenest blade and the highest honour no longer sufficed.

'A chance bullet, coming nobody knows how or from whence, fired perchance by one that fled affrighte at the very flash of his villainous piece, may in a moment put a period to the vastest designs.'

One man who appreciated to the full the value of cannon, and shared in the interest that the renaissance spirit showed in such inventions, was James IV of Scotland. Cannon were not the Scottish monarch's only interest however, he was equally fascinated by ships, tournaments; where he could ride as straight and as hard as any; clothes, he loved finery, music, languages and surgery, he both held a patient and extracted a tooth. Whilst he was not jousting or practising dentistry, James proved a keen administrator and a genuine benefactor to his backward and generally impoverished people. He encouraged a little of the renaissance sun, that was burning so brightly in Italy, to filter into his own dark glens.

'He is of noble stature, neither tall nor short, and as handsome in complexion and shape as a man can be . . . His knowledge of languages is wonderful! He is well read in the bible . . . He is a good historian . . . He never cuts his hair or beard it becomes him very well.'

He inspired a genuine loyalty from his people that reached its tragic nadir on the bloody heath by Flodden edge, where, ironically, the administrative and social elite he had done so much to foster perished with him.

It was James' great passion for all things military that sowed the seeds of his own, and a great number of his subjects, destruction. His interest in artillery was intense and by 1508 the Scots were casting their own guns in Edinburgh. Acts were passed to encourage the practise of archery at the expense of more traditional pastimes, such as golf and football. Regular musters were encouraged and the basis of a professional army laid down. In 1502 James was able to send a force of two thousand men to Denmark, and he reduced the dim vastnesses of the highlands and islands by swift campaigns to extend his authority over those parts. One of his greatest dreams was that of a great, unified, European crusade against the infidel. In spite of these aspirations James' first major encounter proved to be his last and if anyone could be held responsible for the destruction of the Scottish host it was he.

Of his conduct in the battle, the Chronicler Edward Hall makes a fair description, which perhaps would serve as well as his epitaph:—

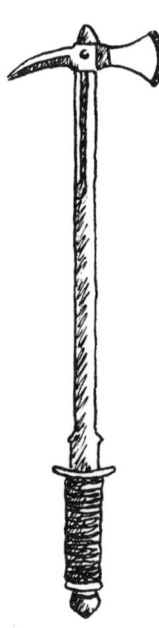

'O, what a noble and triumphant courage was this, for a king to fight in a battle as a mean soldier. But how so ever it happened, God gave the stroke, and he was no more regarded than a poor soldier, for all went one way.'

Long before the march to Flodden, James had quarrelled with the Tudors. As early as 1496 he had championed the dubious cause of the pretender, Perkin Warbeck in his unlikely attempt upon the throne of Henry VII.

By way of support James entered England and ravaged Northumberland, looting, killing and burning. The border holds of Tillmouth, Duddo, Shoreswood, Branxton, Howtell and Lantan were all destroyed.

Horseman's axe
c. 1510.

Warbeck's price for Scottish aid was to have been the surrender of Berwick to the Scots. James proposed that the possession of Berwick should be settled by a single combat between himself and the Earl of Surrey. The Earl, however, had more sense and contemptuously dispersed the Scottish forces, who were besieging Norham. James' campaign had achieved little beyond the ruin of several towers and the cutting of a few throats. Once Henry had dealt with Perkin Warbeck and his somewhat ludicrous aspirations, peace, of a kind, returned to the border.

A further excuse to quarrel arose in 1508 when that notable reiver, the bastard Heron, slew the Scottish warden, Sir Robert Ker, at a truce. The Scotsman's demise seems to have been mourned by few but the slaying of a warden was a serious matter and the affront to national pride was still employed as an excuse for the war of 1513.

In that year England had a king as hungry for glory as his Scottish counterpart, Henry VIII, who was planning to mount an expedition into France in support of the Pope and the Emperor Maximillian. More important than the dignity of his allies was Henry's desire to impress upon the world that England was a first rate power, totally elevated from the feudal mire of the Wars of the Roses.

James, at this time, was married to Henry's sister Margaret but this had not prevented him from renewing the 'Auld Alliance' between Scotland and France, promising mutual aid in the not infrequent event of English aggression.

James may have seen the alliance as a step nearer to his dream of the great crusade. It is a tribute to his naivety that he believed the French would assist in return for help against England. Conversely, the French were over optimistic in hoping that the thrust of a Scottish incursion would keep the English chivalry at home. Such a move had never sufficed before, and was unlikely now to impress. Henry determined upon his jaunt into France. Nevertheless, he did try to extract a guarantee of good behaviour from his brother-in-law. Needless to say, this was not forthcoming.

More tempting to James were the convoys of weaponry and munitions arriving in Scottish ports from France.

In May of 1513 the French queen, subtly playing on James' cavalier notions, sent a 'secret' missive begging him to intercede, if only for her sake. The invitation was accompanied by a further inducement of fourteen thousand crowns.

As the month of June wore on, more and more French vessels were putting into Scottish harbours, bearing more cannon, handguns, pikes and a group of French officers, sent to kick some military sense into James' undisciplined host.

Such obvious preparations were hard to hide and there was little doubt south of the border as to the nature of Scottish intentions. Undeterred, however, Henry, secure as ever in his own considerable arrogance, refused to surrender his designs on France. He did have sufficient sense not to strip the northern counties of able bodied men, and also to entrust the defence of the realm to his ageing but loyal servant Thomas Howard, Earl of Surrey. Despite the weight of his three-score and ten years, Surrey did not waste time in waiting for the Scots to actually attack.

Though the forces he could command were scarcely awe inspiring, the situation was far from being as bad as the ballad makes out

There's none at home left in the land
But jault head months and bursten freers,
Or ragged rustics without rules
Or priests prating for pudding *strives*
Or millners madder than their mules,
Or wanton clerks waking their wives.

There's not a lord left in England,
But all are gane beyond the sea,
Both knight and baron with his band,
With ordinance or artillery.

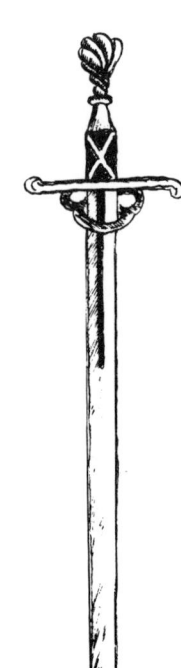

Knight's sword
c. 1520 — note
extra guards for
the hand.

Surrey's preparations were begun before the end of June, though even by the middle of July the situation was still uncertain. Townspeople of the northern burghs began to make good their ancient walls awaiting, in all too familiar dread, the iron shod tramp of Scottish might before their ramparts, the night's skies a blood red flickering beacon of the invaders path.

On 21st July the Earl of Surrey mustered such forces as he would take north at Lambeth. The most significant arm of this nucleus was the artillery train, less impressive on paper than its Scottish counterpart, but destined to be of greater service. In the main it consisted of small two pounders, or 'falcons', and five four pounders or 'Serpentines'. The train was served by an experienced team of some four hundred gunners and drivers.

Meanwhile, north of the border, the pace was also 'hotting up' as James stripped his counties and burghs of men to fill the ranks of his gathering host:—

Each man made haste to mend his gear, . . .
Some made their battle axes bright . . .
Some from their bills did rub the rust . . .
Some made long pikes and lances light . . .

The Scottish herald, Lyon king at arms, was commissioned to carry an ultimatum to Henry at Terouanne in Picardy, which the English were besieging. Delivered on the 26th July, the letter threatened dire consequences for the north of England if the siege, and the whole French escapade along with it, was not abandoned forthwith.

By now Surrey was at Pontefract, where he established a council of war. A system of staging posts and warning beacons was established. Thus, not only could news of any major incursion be relayed, but a rapid summons could be sent out to the shire levies. Throughout the campaign Surrey exudes an aura of calm capability whereas James, for all his zest, seems often over-confident and bombastic.

Some weeks before the main might of the Scottish host was ready to move, Lord Home, with five thousand border lances was already on the offensive, his hard-riding mosstroopers rampaging along the valley of the Till. Replete from this premature orgy of devastation, and doubtless encumbered by their loot, the Scots rode headlong into a well conceived ambush. Concealed in the tall broom of Milfield plain a thousand English longbowmen, under Sir William Bulmer of Brancepeth, waited in deadly earnest. No sooner were the Scots within the trap than the 'cloth yard' rain began to fall, transfixing the raiders in their saddles. As men thudded, writhing or still, into the dust the attack became a rout, the survivors pelting for the border, leaving half a thousand dead and as many prisoners. The English lost no more than sixty, with good cause the road the reivers took was known thereafter as 'the ill-rode'.

Undeterred by this minor reverse, the bulk of the Scottish army continued to assemble. In all, the army numbered nearly sixty thousand, and if numbers alone were not enough, James had also assembled a formidable artillery train. Unlike the comparatively lightweight English version this was a mighty affair. Teams of three dozen oxen were needed to pull each of the heavy sixty pounder siege guns or 'curtals', two, eighteen pounders 'culverins', four, six pounder 'sakers' and six, 'culverins moyenne'.

Despite the impressive array of guns, the gunners themselves were considerably diluted, as many of their number had been sent with the fleet, the gaps in the ranks being filled often by men of limited experience. This, alas, was a serious drawback, the full ramifications of which would only be realised later, though by then it would be too late.

On 22nd August the Scottish army crossed the Tweed at Coldstream. Their crossing was unopposed, and the Scots were soon beneath the walls of Norham, no stranger to attack. But even this proud citadel which, beginning in 1318, had resisted nearly two years of continuous siege, could not withstand the power of the Scottish train. After five days of continuous bombardment, the garrison was surrendered by its castellan, Sir Hugh Cholmeley.

Legend, however, insists that the battle scarred walls of Norham were able even to resist the battering of the guns until an English traitor, doubtless led astray by hopes of vast reward, slipped out of the castle and sought audience with James. This abject creature was able to instruct the Scots in how best to direct their fire, and it was his duplicity that brought about the castle's fall.

Once success was guaranteed James repaid this informant with a rope around his neck.

After the fall of Norham, he moved on along the east bank of the Till and dealt first with Etal, and then Ford. This latter castle became James' headquarters and he made no further move till after the beginning of September.

It has long been asserted that the reason for this dalliance was attributable to the charms of Lady Heron, who was all the more accessible since her unfortunate husband had been carted off to incarceration in Fast Castle, a wild and forbidding coastal fortress. Heron had actually been surrendered as a hostage after his half brother, the celebrated 'bastard', had slain the Scottish warden, as mentioned earlier.

Whether James did prove susceptible is somewhat debatable. Sometime before the Scots arrived Lady Heron had begged assistance for the defence of her home from Surrey who had, in fact, offered to release several important Scottish prisoners, including Lord Johnston and Alexander Home, if Ford were spared.

James appeared indifferent to this chance to redeem his subjects, preferring to storm Ford Castle, in spite of a spirited resistance, which was then pillaged and burnt.

These early successes were of little real consequence, and James' grand invasion had degenerated into little more than a large scale raid, nor were the Scots without problems. Sated by this first orgy of looting, small groups and individuals began to drift away. The highlanders, always fickle in their allegiance, and now short on provisions also, began to disappear. Coupled with this rash of desertions, an outbreak of plague further served to thin out the Scottish host, which had soon lost nearly thirty per cent of its original manpower.

While James dithered at Ford, Surrey began to move. His riders carried news of a general muster in Newcastle, on September 1st, to all the counties of the north. Soon, the men of Lancashire, Cheshire, Yorkshire, Wensleydale and Swaledale were on the move, filling the muddy roads and crumbled lanes with endless columns of armed humanity. The quality of the recruits varied considerably. Surrey's eldest son, who was the Lord Admiral, marched north with one thousand two hundred well drilled marines whose regular transport and fashionable uniforms contrasted sadly with the bulk of the rough county levies, who trudged indifferently in their tangled columns, with shabby clothes and ageing arms. On sight, they would do little to justify the balladeer's confidence:—

All Lancashire, for the most part,
The lusty Stanley stout did lead,
A flock of striplings strong of heart,
Brought up from babes with beef and bred.

On his way to the north Surrey delayed at Durham where he prayed at the shrine of St. Cuthbert and took with him, to Newcastle, the saints banner.

Reviewing the forces he was to command, Surrey must indeed have felt the need for divine assistance. The city was teeming with upwards of twenty eight thousand men, crammed behind her famous walls. Disheartened, disorganised, untrained and unfed this motley host waited for leadership.

Feeling unable to organise within the crowded confines of the town Surrey managed to drag his shambling army northward, to Bolton-in-Glendale, where he was at least able to carry out a proper review and arrange a command structure.

The only good news was the arrival of the admiral and his crack marines, for the rest the Earl was beset by difficulties. He was faced by an enemy vastly superior in numbers, arms and artillery and yet he must engage this enemy without delay, lacking the resources for a protracted campaign. Food was already short and all James had to do was to retire across the border and wait until hunger broke up the English forces; he would then be free to return and ravage the borders at will. Surrey himself felt that it would be folly now to give battle, but the younger men on his staff, Stanley and the Admiral, urged that an encounter was imperative and that somehow the Scots must be brought to battle.

In this end they had one indefatigable ally, King James IV of Scotland.

Knowing his adversaries' unquenchable thirst for glory Surrey resorted to a campaign of calculated insults aimed at his vanity. The dubious honour of conveying these taunts fell to the herald Rouge-Croix who was despatched to Ford where, it was believed, the Scots were still encamped. James, however, was not to be found at Ford. His new position was on the north-eastern slopes of Flodden hill, from where he affirmed to the English herald he was more than willing to give battle but not being totally naive detained Rouge-Croix. Surrey was depending on the messengers's ability to discover something of the Scottish strength. In his place a Scottish herald was sent back to Surrey to relate the King's intentions. Inevitably, this individual was detained by the English.

Believing that the Scots must intend to fight on Milfield plain

Surrey began the protracted task of heaving his cumbersome force onto the march. The English army could scarcely have been an inspiring sight. Apart from the hardcore of professionals from the fleet, the shire levies were as shabby and footsore as ever, though they now had an increasing hunger to contend with. Most of them, apart from Dacre's force of borderers, were a long way from home and marching toward an enemy of uncertain strength. The borderers themselves, astride their shaggy unkempt ponies, were hardly a comforting sight. Scarcely better groomed than their mounts, but armed to the teeth with lances, swords and axe, the borderers exuded an easy confidence and readiness for battle that must have amazed the raw levies from quieter shires.

When the army was finally camped at Wooler, Surrey arranged to exchange Rouge-Croix for his Scottish counterpart, though the news that the herald brought can hardly have made their reunion a joyful one. The picture presented was one of unrelieved gloom for the English — the Scots were encamped in a strong position with considerable numbers, well fed, well armed and backed by their formidable artillery. The guns were dug into position covering the passage between the east end of Flodden hill and the line of the Till. This low-lying track of near morass was the only approach to the Scottish position, but any attempt to advance could be enfilladed devastating fire from the cannon above.

Such news could scarcely suffice to gladden the heart of even the most optimistic commander and, as Surrey and his despondent officers reviewed their situation, in the rain at Wooler, there seemed little cause for optimism.

As the men crouched wearily around their sodden bivouacs, depressed and enfeebled by cold, wet and hunger, rumours about the impregnable position and formidable strength of their enemy, inevitably began to filter down. Morale, which had never been high, had reached its nadir.

The only immediate solution Surrey and his staff could think of was to intensify the campaign of abuse and draw James, through rage, down from his position of strength. Despite the best endeavours of the redoubtable Rouge-Croix, James had more sense than to budge.

Legend relates that on the night of 7th September, as Surrey and his council sat in damp despair, the English camp was galvanised into sudden near-panic by the abrupt arrival of a squadron of unidentified horsemen, Well mounted and heavily armed, they clattered into the midst of the encampment. Not apparently one to stand on formality, the leader of this stalwart band thrust his way, unannounced, into the council tent itself. Only when he stood before the Earl himself, did he deign to remove his visored helmet. The countenance thus revealed was that of John Heron, he that had slain the Scottish warden, and harried the borders ever since. Despite his wild reputation and the price upon his head, Surrey was in no position to argue technicalities. Without further ado the erstwhile outlaw and his confederates, all men of similar stamp, were enrolled into the English army.

Legend further insists that it was Heron who suggested the decisive flanking march that so affected the outcome of the battle. Whether or not this is true is, and will always be, debatable.

What is certain however, is that the following morning the camp at Wooler was struck, the Till was forded and a northward march on the western bank begun.

This whole manoeuvre was conducted in full view of the Scottish host who, though doubtless amused at first by the ant-like scurryings of their foes below, must have become increasingly baffled, and then concerned. The English army marched steadily northward, past Doddington, where the ground rose to the heather clad moor and then finally out of sight altogether.

The obvious conclusions were that, either the English were about to mount an invasion of their own, or this was a ruse designed to panic the Scots into abandoning their position. Some of the nobility were for an immediate return to Scotland but James preferred to remain and await developments.

In fact the English had only proceeded as far as was necessary to conceal their camp from the straining eyes of the Scots. The bulk of Watch Law, reposed between the two armies, effectively guaranteed concealment. As darkness fell the admiral and some of his officers trekked to the summit of Watch Law to review the enemy position from this northward vantage.

The Scottish position now lay to the south, atop and beyond Branxton Hill. Though steep, the climb here was at least free from artillery bombardment. An English advance from the present northerly position might tempt the Scots into an attack, as they must either fight or submit to having their lines of communication and withdrawal irretrievably severed.

This meant that the weary English must once again splash across the Till, but by first light on the 9th Surrey's army was on the move, bearing only their arms; pots, pans, tents and baggage were abandoned. As there was no food anyway this was no great sacrifice, and if defeat were to follow then there would be few returning. Surrey had run out of options and was chancing everything on this last gambit. Failure against such odds could only mean disaster. The English army that marched upon Branxholm had to win through, or perish in the attempt.

Before the English could even begin to come to grips with their

Scottish foes they had first to contend with the forces of nature, more particularly the sluggish waters of the Till. The narrow bridge at Twizel could not accommodate the vast array of men, horses and guns, and whilst the van under the admiral crossed by this route, Surrey led the main body across the shallows at Mill-Ford. Even with the numbers thus divided, it took the admiral a full hour to get his forces over the water. Though narrow, the bridge was, and not as stated in the ballad, invisible from the Scots position, as indeed was the ford, so that the Scots were blissfully unaware of their impending nemesis.

Once the tortuous crossing was accomplished the English host was bullied and marshalled into full line of battle. Thus arrayed, the advance continued. Though the army had decamped at first light it was not until 1 p.m. that the alarm was first raised in the Scottish camp.

> From Flodden ridge,
> The Scots beheld the English host,
> Leave Barmoor Wood, their evening post,
> And heldful watched them as they crossed.
> The Till by Twizel Bridge.

Once the approach of the English became certain James set about preparing a suitable welcome. As usual he was at variance with numerous of his lords, but promptly threw a violent tantrum when any mention of retreat was made. Thus resolved, the Scots began the cumbersome task of transferring their position, about a mile to the north and deploying along the top of Branxton Hill, dragging those guns that could be shifted with them. This movement, once completed, gave the advancing English the unenviable task of charging uphill against a numerically superior foe, both well rested and well fed.

Even as they clambered up the tussocky slope Surrey's weary troops would be lashed by a storm of Scottish lead. If, upon reaching the bottom of the hill, the English either declined to attack or their attempt foundered, the Scots were in an ideal position to swoop down upon them with terrible momentum.

Forming up in the dip, out of sight of the English, the Scottish line comprised; on the left Home and Huntly's contingent, then the division of Errol, Crawford and Montrose. In the centre stood the King's division with the wild highlanders of Lennox and Argyle on the right. A fifth division commanded by the Earl of Bothwell was left as a reserve. The lowland divisions were captained by French officers, who were responsible for the organisation of the pike columns, that had replaced the old schiltroms. Ironically, those few Frenchmen who survived the ensuing carnage were done to death by their erstwhile charges as being the architects of their defeat.

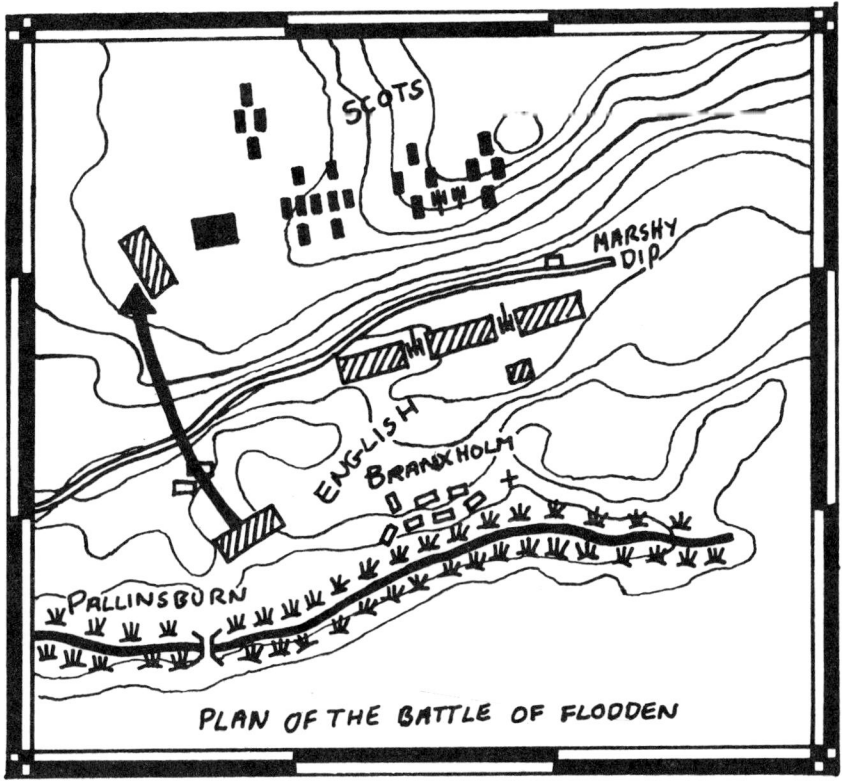

PLAN OF THE BATTLE OF FLODDEN

As the massed ranks of the Scottish army were being pressed into formation James' gunners, cursed, sweated and heaved to first dig free, and then manhandle, the unwieldy pieces to their new position. Again, at this same time, the rabble of camp followers began burning the heaped refuse created by the host. Thus the final manoeuverings of both sides were obscured from the other by the huge and ominous pall of filthy smoke, emanating from the abandoned camp. There could hardly have been a more fitting omen. Unaware of, and thus undaunted by, the reception being prepared above, the English continued stolidly in their advance. Plodging through the soft clay around the Pallinsburn, the guns had to be temporarily abandoned as the ground was too soft. Whilst an easier alternative was sought the van pressed on, trudging up the incline that brought them clear of the Pallinsburn, and gave them, at last, the first clear sight of their enemy. It was far from encouraging.

Perched in massive concentration along the summit of Branxton Hill, the ranks of Scottish pikemen waited, like some giant hedgehog, their line ablaze with proud surcoats and fluttering banners. The army must have seemed to fill the skyline in a great surge of menacing strength.

Already the admiral had come too far. His van had so far out-stripped the rearguard and the cumbersome artillery, that any sudden rush from the daunting host would surely sweep his slender forces back into the mire.

Despite the mere few hundred yards that separated the two armies, the admiral kept his head and marched his vanguard along the southern bank of the Pallinsburn. He could not but help be aware how tempting a target his comparatively small force must be. Any moment the English must have expected a sudden, deafening chorus of Scottish war cries and the stomach turning realisation of their own vulnerability. But the attack never came. Whether the target was not sufficiently tempting to make James abandon his position of strength, or whether his own vainglorious chivalry forbad the descent upon such an unequal foe, we shall never know.

Though the admiral had managed to preserve a bold face he had all the while been sending frantic messages to Surrey, begging him to make haste. At length, the bulk of the army, along with the cumbersome artillery, was able to come up and with their foes arrayed impressively before, the English were drawn up to meet them. The right wing was commanded by Edmund Howard, Surrey's third son, and it was with the right that Surrey was particularly concerned. Three thousand odd raw levies, mostly from Lancashire and Cheshire, bolstered by a few Howard retainers and the hardcore of knights in their midst, such as the doughty Bryan Tunstall. Between the various bodies of infantry, the English guns were positioned. They were not long idle.

As the English line began to move out of the Pallinsburn valley they were greeted by a hail of Scottish fire, and the battle of Flodden was begun with a furious artillery duel.

It would seem, superficially, that all the odds must lie with the Scots but this was not, in fact, the case. Not only were the heavier guns much harder to manoeuvre but the simple elevating mechanisms made downhill fire surprisingly difficult. Perhaps most telling of all, it was now that the inexperience of the bulk of the Scottish gunners began to show.

Coolly directed by Sir Nicholas Appleyard and William Blakenall, the English gunners methodically raked the Scottish batteries, smashing man and cannon alike into mangled oblivion. With terrible precision the pride of James' army was hammered into fatal silence. Having dealt with the guns, the English fire was now directed onto the inert masses of Scottish infantry, so obligingly outlined upon the horizon. A storm of iron shot rained upon the helpless ranks, pummelling bloody, gaping holes, killing and maiming. Soon, the

Battle of Flodden.

haughty lines of spearmen reeled under the relentless holocaust of shot lashing their hilltop position.

As their artillery kept the enemies attention more than occupied, the English advanced stolidly till they were almost at the base of the hill. The extreme left was held by the redoubtable Edward Stanley. Surrey in the centre, was faced with a fairly sharp decline dropping to a mire. This was to be of considerable importance, for the Scots, in order to attack, would have to cross the mire and advance up the incline, thus losing most of the momentum of their sweep down the hillside.

Whatever James' faults, he was never indecisive, and was not the man to stand idly by and see his army decimated. Nor was he prepared to wait until the English reached his position. For a man of James' temperament there was only one alternative — attack.

As Surrey feared, James had perceived the weakness of the English right, aggravated by the temporary desertion of Dacre's horse, their mounts panicked into flight by the unfamiliar noise of the guns. Now Howard's raw troops, unnerved by the chaos amongst the cavalry, had to face the daunting spectacle of ten thousand wild borderers under Home and Huntly descending upon them. It was altogether too much. Stirrings of panic in the ranks, at first as gentle as the rippling waves fanned by a summer breeze, soon swelled to a cascade of fleeing men, scattering and stumbling in blind disorder. Those few who dared stand firm were swept away in a deluge of border pikes, too few to even check the thousands pouring down upon the English right.

Jubilant at this early success, James prepared to personally lead the triumphant advance of his own central division. This ultimate act of folly, throwing all idea of generalship to the wind for the dream of personal glory, provoked the customary storm of concern from his lordly advisors. Equally customarily, it was disregarded and James prepared to rush to his doom, Scotland's renaissance hero about to make the final sacrifice to his own quixotic vanity. Practically, it was a frightful blunder to deprive the army of effective leadership — its King becoming little more than a common footsoldier. With no single commander able to control the overall situation the Scottish host degenerated into a flailing juggernaut, steered inexorably onto the course of its own destruction.

James' recklessness was scant encouragement to those few who stood firm on the English right. One of these few alas, the stalwart Bryan Tunstall who, hewing madly at the onrushing Scots, slew Sir Malcolm McKeen and several others before he was overpowered and slain.

> But up to heaven with angels bright
> His golden ghost did flick'ring fly.

Soon, Edmund Howard, supported by only a small band of retainers found himself surrounded. Fighting desperately, hemmed in on all sides by their foe, the English fought with despairing courage, dropping one by one until Howard himself was the only survivor.

Such an important knight would inevitably bring a hefty ransom and was therefore worth considerably more alive. These economic considerations were ever uppermost in the minds of the borderers. Nevertheless, Howard continued to fight, striking down all who dared approach. It seemed that all was now up for the English on the right but at that precise moment, in a manner that would bring joy to the heart of any Hollywood producer, Dacre's border horse sped swiftly to the rescue.

Though considerably inferior to the Scots in numbers, the English enjoyed the tremendous advantage of being both fresh and mounted. Well armed and born to fight, borderer fought borderer in deadly earnest.

At least the affray was more or less in deadly earnest. The underlying pragmatism that marked the borderers' code of survival did not rate international differences as weighty enough to necessitate a fight to the death. Therefore, after a brief but bloody clash the two forces, as if by tacit agreement, drew apart and faced each other with sullen hostility.

Neither Home nor Dacre would ever admit to any 'arrangement' at this point, though neither was destined to play any further role in the battle.

In the chaos of the initial charge, the bastard Heron, with his own select troop of cut-throats, had hacked a bloody path through Home's division to rescue the beleaguered Howard. Their mission accomplished, they cut an equally bloody swathe through the Scottish ranks to reach Surrey's division, slaying Sir Davy Home and numerous of his troop *en route*.

The situation on the right had, thus resolved into a stalemate, something of a 'Mexican stand-off'. Though the English right had been broken, Dacre's horse now solidly filled the vacuum and Home's division, satisfied with their efforts to date, retired back to the hill to their previous position.

However, few in the English centre had long to ponder over the situation on the right. The daunting sight of King James' division sweeping down upon them *en masse* was enough to guarantee the full attention of even the coolest warrior.

As the Scots descended, the English longbowmen stepped forward and the familiar rain of death began to whistle down upon the advancing mass. The Scots had long had cause to fear the terrible 'cloth yard' shaft but James had at least learned something from a litany of earlier defeats.

Only too well aware that his proud army could easily end up in row upon row of studded corpses, he had provided his front ranks with heavy wooden shields, or pavises, which could be raised by the holders as a protective screen and then discarded, when the armies finally closed. Thus, the arrow storm had less effect than in previous encounters. Though Scots did fall, the customary wholesale slaughter was avoided and the rush of the advance remained unchecked.

> The English shafts in volleys hail'd
> In headlong charge their horse assailed;
> Front, flank and rear, their squadrons sweep
> To break the Scottish circle deep,
> That fought around their king
> But yet, though thick the shafts as snow,
> Through charging knights like whirlwinds go,
> Though bill-men ply the ghastly blow
> Unbroken was the ring.

The marsh into which the Scots descended undoubtedly came as a considerable surprise, as also would the ensuing uphill climb to finally reach the English. The terrible momentum, which was meant to smash through the inert ranks of the English, was irretrievably lost and the charge ended on a significantly lame note.

Once the two lines were finally engaged, the serious business of killing commenced. Now the Scots began, too late, to discover how stiff and unwieldy a weapon their long pikes were. Though ideal for the smashing, grinding impact of the initial charge, in the cut and thrust of protracted hand to hand, they were proving totally inferior to the bills borne by the English.

The English bill was a hybrid of the battlefield, born of a lethal union between an agricultural implement, the bill-hook, and the military spear. Originally the peasants hook became mounted upon a long pole until, around 1300, the two weapons were fused to create a ghastly martial instrument sporting a blade, with a long spear-like head to the fore and a shorter narrow edge at the back. Far lighter and more versatile than the cumbersome pike, Surrey's troopers were able to lop off the the heads of their enemies' weapons, and then hack them down in a barbaric ritual of slaughter that was now being enacted at the foot of Branxton Hill. Thoughts of hunger and fatigue were swept away in the rush of adrenalin as the English fought back savagely. Too outnumbered to consider giving quarter, they began to carve bloody gaps in the Scottish ranks.

No sooner had Surrey engaged the King's division than the division commanded by Errol, Crawford and Montrose swept down upon the Admiral's contingent. Here, the pattern was the same, muddled and disordered by the downhill rush, the Scots lacked the close packed concentration needed to burst through the ranks on impact. Instead, they too became embroiled in a slogging killing match, where the Scottish pike was running a poor second. With methodical precision the Admiral's professional soldiers hacked, slashed and hewed, piling the Scottish dead in heaps. With terrible tenacity the English held their ground and slowed the Scottish advance in a welter of dead. Confused and disheartened, the Scots of this division began to lose heart, to falter and then to run. At first a trickle, and then a torrent, the Scotsmen fled. None of the three earls that had led them was alive to witness the disgrace.

Up to now the English had been desperately on the defensive against the might of the Scottish onslaught, beefed up by their superior numbers. Now the field was already thickening with Scottish dead. Many had fled, leaving the King's division to face both Surrey and the Admiral. At last, the pendulum had swung to favour the English. At last, the Scottish foe had been levelled. The fear, hunger and despair that had haunted Surrey's army for so long was to be washed away in a torrent of Scottish blood. Many of the nobility had already succumbed to the slashing bills. The Scottish position had sunk from certain victory to equal contest and finally, to a desperate bid for survival. The slaughter was to drag on for another two hours but even the arrival of Bothwell's reserve, (and it seems questionable whether this reserve was ever actually committed), could not stem the tide of disaster.

James, sensing that the game was up, resolved to make one last suicidal bid for glory, the quixotic 'grand geste' preferable at least to facing the enormity of his defeat. With the tattered survivors of his household around him, he launched a berserk charge against the banners of Surrey himself, finally falling in a welter of gore, his retainers around him, scarcely a stonesthrow from the Earl's position. One legend, at least, claims that the doughty Earl himself laid low the Scottish monarch in the final confrontation. However he finally met his end. James died as he had led, like a common soldier, the significance of his passing ignored in the frenzied carnage. Cut and slashed by bills, the King fell almost unnoticed as his men, now too occupied by the pressing problem of their own survival, fought despairingly in the gathering dusk.

Where was the Scottish right? The division of highlanders under Argyle and Lennox whose numbers, even yet, could stem the tide of defeat. The highlanders had problems of their own. Chief among these was the redoubtable Sir Edward Stanley who, rather than wait for the Scots to descend into the fray, had carried the fray to meet them.

At this time Argyle and Lennox were preparing to advance and rescue the King whose own precipitate recklessness had deprived them of firm command. Stanley's men swarmed up the north-eastern slopes of the hill. Although not easy, the route was invisible to the Scots who only became aware of the unexpected English presence when showers of arrows thudded into their ranks. The lightly armed highlanders dropped in scores and their discomfiture was completed when the English knights and men-at-arms crashed into their midst. The contest was short and sharp, the English fighting with a sustained ferocity that soon sapped the sagging morale of the stunned highlanders.

Both Argyle and Lennox, in the company of several notable chiefs, fell in a desperate attempt to rally their men. Their leaders fallen, panic spread like wildfire amongst the highlanders, and soon they were streaming downhill. Ironically, their flight must have taken them past the bodies of their king and his household. The highlanders never paused to look.

The now scattered highlanders had been the last hope of salvation for the struggling survivors in the Scottish centre. The slaughter went on into the twilight, ever decreasing bands of Scots vainly trying to parry the frenzied slashing of the English, now so drunk with blood-lust that even those too wounded to rise, or who were begging quarter, were not spared.

The only faint chance remaining was the bloodied, but still intact division of Home and Huntly. The latter was anxious to advance but the former declined, too pragmatic to squander his force in such a vain endeavour. Home saw his duty to the border as far outweighing his duty to the king. With his command, at least, intact Home would have some chance of resisting the storm that would break upon the border, once the Scots were defeated.

At last the darkness halted the massive slaughter. Dawn revealed a scene of hideous carnage. Surrey's army had accounted for some ten thousand Scots, including the flower of their chivalry. One archbishop, one bishop, ten earls, nineteen barons, three hundred knights. Whole glens and towns were stripped of the cream of their manhood and joined their renaissance prince in a death more typical of a Dark Age hero.

The English gained a great haul of booty from the mass of Scottish slain and their abandoned camp. The pride of James' army, his great artillery train, fell into English hands. Henry VIII was quick to shower his victorious captains with honours, Surrey became Duke of Norfolk, the Admiral now being created Earl of Surrey. Sir Edward Stanley was made Lord Monteagle.

The host that had defeated the Scots had lost some one thousand seven hundred men in the battle, and of those that survived, only four thousand four hundred, under Dacre, remained in arms, to harry the Scottish Marches.

On the morning after the battle a half naked corpse was dragged from the macabre pile of Scottish dead. Taken to Berwick, this was formally recognised as the mortal remains of James IV of Scotland. The body was disembowelled, embalmed and then sent, first to Newcastle and then in a lead casket to London. Henry's Queen Catherine debated sending the grisly trophy to her husband in France, but finally sent his bloody surcoat instead.

The remains proceeded through successive stages of degradation. At first housed in the monastery of Sheen, it was thrown into a lumber room when the dissolution took place. Still later, workmen in the house cut off the head and used it for a macabre plaything. Thereafter it came into possession of Lancelot Young, Elizabeth I's master glazier, who kept it on display at his home. Eventually it was buried in an anonymous grave.

The site is today marked by a large stone memorial, whose location, however does not really give any real impression of the battlefield. Take a loop from the A697 through Flodden itself and west into Branxton, the road bisects the English and Scots position — only a hedge now marks the line of the marsh so fatal to the Scots.

Chapter Six

RAIDS AND REIVERS

For many years the reiver enjoyed the romantic image of the 'Young Lochinvar' tradition — a dashing rogue pounding across moonlit moors with his stolen bride upon his fiery steed. A far more objective approach, by modern historians, has rather dulled this image and the reiver now emerges as a scruffy peasant farmer cum bandit stealing over the mosses, mounted on a shaggy, underfed garron. With this, however, must come a measure of respect for the reiver, both as a natural survivor in a hostile land, and as an accomplished and resourceful guerilla.

The term 'reiver' could equally be applied to any person living in northern England or southern Scotland and, although the prize for notoriety must go to the inhabitants of Liddlesdale, the Elliots, Armstrongs, Bells and Croziers, their Northumbrian contemporaries were as lawless. The border was unsettled right throughout the Middle Ages, but the real era of the reiver was during the 16th Century, until the union of the crowns, in 1603, saw a major, determined and successful attempt by James I to bring law and order to both sides of the line. The Northumbrian 'Riding' clans, Charltons, Robsons, Ridleys and several others were as prone to the bloody idea of the feud or 'feid' as any Scotsman, and Northumbrian history of the period contains many desperate and bloody encounters fought in the name of family honour. The strict law against intermarriage between the English and Scots, the constant border wars, major incursions and endless forays did not, surprisingly enough, prevent constant intermarriage across the border. This was often the most sure means of ending a protracted feud. Furthermore, despite any natural antipathy, borderers of both nationalities would always combine to defeat and frustrate attempts to bring law and order by either government. The reiver was, nominally, a farmer though he would generally prefer to be relieving others of their stock than tending to his own. The most suitable time of year for this clandestine occupation was in the autumn, when the summer sun had partially dried out the mosses and the gathering nights afforded better cover. An expedition could involve anything from a few to a thousand men and could penetrate seventy miles into hostile country, often lifting all the stock in the afflicted area.

Aside from his native wit and low cunning, the reiver had to place great reliance upon his horse, which had to be suited to the dangerous mosses and the arduous business of driving cattle. The sturdy galloway was the favoured beast. The reivers of Northumberland were capable, when mounted, of holding their own against any contemporary conventional force.

As well as choosing his mount with care the reiver would need to be equally circumspect in his choice of arms. He might have to fight on foot or on horseback, he must fear arrows, lances, swinging broadswords and latterly, flying lead. The border laws required every able-bodied man to appear with his own arms on 'Muster Days' — the object of which was to attempt to drill the borderers against invasions. Though these musters were regarded as something of a standing joke by most, they do provide a record of the appearance and arms carried by those, who on less official occasions, were wont to mount invasions of their own, at which time they were generally less available for observation and record.

A muster in Northumberland in 1584 showed that the Northumbrians still relied upon the longbow. An earlier muster-roll, from further west, described the appearance of those present in greater detail 'with steel caps and jacks'. A jack or 'brigandine' was the poor man's answer to plate armour, and consisted of a garment quilted and stuffed, faced with cowhide, sewn with metal plates or studs. This could be combined with a mail shirt worn underneath.

A more fortunate or wealthy individual could afford breast and back plates. Leg armour was scarce, protection to the extremities being more usually afforded by heavy leather riding boots. Helmets could consist of a simple metal skull cap or be of the type known as a sallet which afforded some protection to the neck. As the 16th Century progressed the more substantial morion and 'lobster pot' styles appeared. A Scottish ordinance of 1540 records the following appearance, which, it is submitted, would differ only slightly south of the Tweed:—

'Unladen gentlemen and yeomen have jacks of plate, Halbriks, splents, sallet or steel bonnet with pesanor gorget and all to wear swords.'

The Bishop of Durham described the reiver in the following manner.

'Wearing a steel cap, a coat of plate, stockings of plate, bootes and spurres; a skottish short sworde and a dagger, a horsemans staffe and a case of pistolls.'

The 'Staffe' mentioned above is a type of long handled battleaxe. A reiver would be more likely to carry a border lance, its timber shaft tipped with steel. This implement, besides being useful for impaling your opponents and prodding recalcitrant beasts, could also be gainfully employed on the hot trod whereby any man with a lighted peat on the point of his lance could legally cross the border in pursuit of lifted beasts.

The advance of the Sixteenth Century saw a decline in the use of the heavy, long, double-handed sword and the appearance of the lighter, semi-basket hilted weapon, far more suitable for the horseman. A fine example survives in the museum at Hawick, said once to have belonged to the celebrated reiver Johnnie Armstrong of Gilnockie. The longbow still retained its traditional popularity in England, though the cross-bow, or the more primitive latch, was always more favoured by the Scots.

Firearms, of the early matchlock type, were around, though by no means universal, towards the end of the era. Matchlock carbines, or calivers, were in use, but the lighted match needed to operate these early black-powder pieces was an obvious disadvantage, in an occupation where stealth and surprise were the determining factors in life expectancy. Furthermore, the slow rate of fire and susceptibility to

Hepburn Bastle near Eglingham.

124

damp of these weapons also reduced their value. The more sophisticated wheel-lock, characteristic of the 'daggs' or pistols of the period was more reliable and more discreet. It was also far more expensive, only a gentleman could hope, lawfully, to acquire a pair.

These, apart from home-made dirks and fighting knives, were the basic tools our ancestors required for survival, and perhaps of all these, the lance would be most favoured as the all-round weapon. Thieves and bandits they may have been but any army would have been glad of them.

Grindon Rig 1558, NT931437.

'They sally out of their own borders, in the night, in troops, through unfrequented by-ways, and many intricate windings. All the day time, they refresh themselves and their horses, in lurking holes they had pitched upon before, till they arrive in the dark at those places they have a design upon. As soon as they have seized upon the booty, they in like manner, return home in the night, through blind ways, and fetching many a compass. The more skilful any captain is to pass through those wild deserts, crooked turnings, and deep precipices, in the thickest mists and darkness, his reputation is the greater, and he is looked upon as a man of an excellent head.'

Bishop Leslie.

A few miles south of Norham stand the famous Duddo Stones, a group of prehistoric monoliths, redolent with all of the mystery and romance that clings to such ancient places. Arranged in a rough circle, some thirty feet in diameter, fine large stones stand in impressive isolation; it is generally accepted that the date of their erection lies sometime between 1600-1000 B.C. Atop their own small eminence, these silent sentinels have stood throughout the centuries, whilst their original builder has vanished in the dark shroud of prehistory.

When the first Elizabeth, free at last of her much unlamented sister ascended the throne in 1558 the stones were already cloaked with the mantle of great age. Their solitude was enlivened in that year, however, by an encounter which was to become known as the affair of Grindon Rig.

The Scots welcomed the monarch to the throne by unleashing an unusually savage spate of raids and forays, the clash and clangour of steel upon steel was heard even more than usual. One of the large incursions was mounted by a mixed body of horse and foot, the former believed to number around a thousand, and was led by French officers. Replete from their widespread reiving, the raiders were almost in sight of the Tweed when an English force, under Sir Henry Percy, overtook the overburdened column and fell upon them with a vengeance.

The affray seems to have been that kind of savage, lightning strike at which all borderers excelled, a swirling thrusting mêlée, long Northumbrian lances darting and spitting with lethal precision into the surprised mass of Scots. The hapless French officers could never have dreamed of such combat, being more accustomed to the ponderous, clumsy warfare on the field of battle.

Details of the engagement are inevitably vague but is certain that the Scots were utterly routed. The action is said to have begun about a mile, or a mile and a half, north west of Duddo, the defeated Scots fleeing towards the fords over the Till or Twizel bridge, though they were harassed all the way back to the Tweed itself.

Though complete, the English victory was not gained without some loss, one definite loser was William Clavering, the son of Robert Clavering of Callaly. William seems to have been the laird of nearby Duddo tower to where he was carried back from the fray 'so very craysed and sore wounded' that he barely had time to sign his will before expiring.

The Raid of the Reidswire, 1575.

> The seventh of July the smith to say,
> At the Reidswire the tryst was set;
> Our wardens they affixed the day
> And as they promised, so they met.
> Alas that day I'll ne'er forgett!
> Was sure sae feard, ad then sae faire
> They came theare justice for to gett,
> Will never green to come again.

The fight happened on the watershed, some three miles north east of Carter Bar, which is a 'swire' or strip of land that links Catcleugh Shin and Arks Edge. The impressive sweep of tussocky rolling hills, that opens out below, once over the weary climb to the summit northward from the A696. The road itself is not easily forgotten when wintry conditions persist.

Nearly two centuries before the famous raid, English and Scots had clashed bloodily on Carter Fell when, in 1400, Sir Robert Umfraville decisively smashed a substantial raiding party.

The encounter discussed at present is remarkable in that it took place upon a "truce" day, usually one of the few times at which the turbulent borderers could be relied upon to behave themselves, and to keep the peace rather than break it. It was an established border custom that on these occasions the border wardens could meet and settle any outstanding disputes, hopefully without the more usual breaking of heads.

On the particular and fateful day in question, the English warden, Sir John Forster, met with his Scottish counterpart Sir John Carmichael, the keeper of Liddlesdale. The meeting was fixed for July 7th and for a while the business of the day appeared to go smoothly, but after three hours or so of amiable discourse, the situation took a distinct turn for the worse.

Earlier in the same year the fiery Fenwicks had raided into the equally tempestuous realm of Liddlesdale, the excuse for the foray being the slaying of one of their number by a Liddlesdale man, notwithstanding the fact that the killing had occurred over a generation before. Shortly after the raid Carmichael had obtained the custody of one of the alleged perpetrators from Sir George Heron but Forster now appeared at the truce-day in place of his dis-favoured subordinate.

The English warden appears as a singularly unattractive and unpopular character. He was well known for his many illegal ventures, furthermore his arrogance and condescension had not endeared him to his contemporaries. Forsters' general tone and attitude seem to have become increasingly vexatious to Carmichael, who resented being reminded of his inferior status! The general level of tension, always present when English and Scots met, was continually exacerbated by the vast amounts of alcohol consumed at these meetings. All this, added to the fact that both the Fenwicks and the Liddlesdale Croziers were out in force, meant that the whole situation was a virtual powder keg and all that was now needed was the spark. As yet no blows had been struck and the presentation of bills continued, until one was laid against a notorious English thief named Farnstein. For some reason, best known only to himself, Forster chose to prevaricate over this particular bill, to Carmichael's rising fury. When polite remonstrations failed, anger and then abuse followed, finally degenerating into a slanging match as Englishman and Scot abandoned protocol and traded insult for insult.

The new mood of hostility released the latent enmity between Croziers and Fenwicks, first insults then arrows flew; William Fenwick of Wallington crumpled beneath a Scottish shaft:—

> Carmichael then speak out plainlike
> And cloke no cause for ill or good;
> The other answering him as vainlie

Began to reckon kin and blood
He raise and raxed him where he stood
And bade him match him with his marrows.
Then Tindaill heard them reasun rude,
And they loot off a feight of arrows.

The sudden upsurge of violence was enough to shock both officials into some degree of sensibility, and both attempted to restrain the fraying tempers of their hot blooded compatriots. Ostensibly making an effort to restore order Carmichael drifted away from the English warden and his party, who were instantly set upon by a substantial body of Scotsmen. As it was a truce day the English were unarmoured and generally unprepared, thus virtually defenceless as the mass descended upon them. In the tawdry mêlée that followed Sir George Heron was slain but the Scots were worsted in a murderous counter-attack mounted by the outraged Tynedale men.

For a while it seemed that the day must go against the Scots, but the timely and unexpected arrival of a substantial body of latecomers began to tip the balance in their favour.

Finally the English were routed and a running fight ensued as the pursuit was carried southward for a good three miles. All in all the affray had been a bloody one, many had fallen on both sides and many more would carry scars of the fray till their dying day. Unwounded, other than in terms of vanity, Sir John Forster had to suffer the indignity of being made captive, alongside many officers from the English side, including Cuthbert Collingwood and Francis Russell.

With help of God the game gald right
Fra time the foremost of them fell;
Then ower the know, without goodnight,
They ran with mony a shout and yell.

Although the Reidswire technically ranks as a Scottish victory, the affray was something of an embarrassment to the court in Edinburgh who were anxious to avoid any form of confrontation with England. As a result the pristoners were treated with every courtesy and in fact were soon restored to their liberty, ironically the Scots chose to hand over Carmichael himself as a pledge.

Thus the incident passed without any further, more serious, outbreaks of violence. Sir John Forster inevitably protested long and loud but few were ignorant of the true nature of his character and his splutterings went unheeded. Needless to say, however, this temporary buffet to law and order gave rise to a sharp increase in reiving and raiding, not that this was anything new on the borders.

Sir John's attendance at Truce days seemed dogged by misadventure, no doubt that is how he would have preferred to describe it. Ten years after the Reidswire incident in July 1585, Forster was one of the principals in yet another border drama.

This later incident occurred on Wyndygyle, some miles west of Carter Bar, though the exact details of the fracas are unclear as neither of the principal protagonists was renowned for his veracity. The Scottish warden in this instance was one Thomas Ker of Ferniehirst, a suitable candidate for any form of mayhem, a noted reiver and free booter, who was currently enjoying a celebrated vendetta against the worthy citizens of Jedburgh.

Accompanying Forster was his son-in-law Lord Francis Russell though his presence was contrary to his relative's wishes, the warden was convinced that Ker bore Russell a grudge and would not be deterred from violence by the mere formalities of the truce day. For once Forster's advices seem to have been founded, at least in part, in fact.

Nonetheless, Russell insisted on attending the truce which began in an air of uneasy calm, soon disturbed by a series of random scuffles. In the midst of these petty disturbances a shot rang out and Russell was mortally wounded. Surprisingly, the murder did not result in a full scale affray, the killing seems to have had a sobering effect on those present and once pledges were exchanged the meeting broke up without further bloodshed. The perpetrator of the slaying, together with the precise motive, remain shrouded in mystery.

Later, Forster was to claim that the attack was wholly premeditated, that the Scots had come in full armour and armed to the teeth. He further claimed to have been pursued for nearly four miles after Russell's death by the blood crazed Scottish hordes, the fatal shot also having served as a signal for a massed charge. Predictably Ferniehirst's version was entirely conflicting and the full truth of the incident will never be known and no culprit was ever caught or even named.

The spectacular scenery of Carter Fell and the border fence is amongst the most awesome in the region, harshly forbidding in the biting winter winds, obscured by drifting snows and clogging mists. Even in the summer months the landscape is never soft, the empty rolling hills extend to the far horizon where only the haunting cry of the curlew punctures the perfect calm.

Westward there is a rude stone cairn upon Wyndygyle that marks the alleged spot where Russell fell. The Reidswire is commemorated in more dramatic style by an annual ride with horsemen from both sides of the border.

The motorist need do no more than ascend Carter Fell by the A696 and pull in at the summit layby to appreciate the nature of the ground.

The Raid on Haydon Bridge, 1587.

O Have ye na heard o' the fause Salkelde?
O Have ye na heard o' the keen lord Scrope?
How they hae ta'en bould Kinmont Willie,
On Haribee to hang him up.

Kinmont Willie

William Armstrong of Morton Rigg, known to border legend as Kinmont Willie — was an experienced Liddlesdale thug with a formidable list of raids, pillagings and murders to his credit. He is most famous perhaps, as a major, albeit totally unwilling, protagonist in the events that led up the celebrated raid upon Carlisle Castle. Willie, who had frustrated all attempts by the English West March Wardens to end his depredations was finally taken by Lord Scrope on a truce day, a desperate expedient and a gross violation of border custom. Despite a spirited resistance, against hopeless odds, the reiver was taken in chains to Carlisle, and there incarcerated pending his inevitable appointment with the hangman. It was from that formidable bastion that he was rescued in a daring commando style exploit, engineered and led by the Bold Buccleuch, that redoubtable and spirited keeper of Liddlesdale, himself a noted exponent of the reiver's art.

This all happened in 1596, nearly ten years after Kinmont had led his freebooting border clansman in the 'taking up' of Haydon Bridge. The trial and execution of Mary Queen of Scots in early 1587 had, not unnaturally, prompted her son James VI to a loud but somewhat hollow burst of protest, enough to proclaim his outrage at his late mother's untimely end without adversely affecting his chances of gaining the succession from Elizabeth. The standard of righteous indignation was kept admirably aloft by the borderers themselves who were quick to take advantage of the tension and step up their predatory forays against the English foe. One of the more notable and best recorded incursions was the descent upon Haydon Bridge.

A body of around four hundred riders, drawn from the hardy reiving stock of Liddlesdale, Ewesdale, Eskdale and Annandale were involved. One route the Scots may have followed traversed the border line by the desolate head of the Liddle water itself and then followed the North Tyne by the heights of Black Knowe, Rough Pike and the Rigg, skirting the Bewcastle area and Spadeadam Waste.

It is more likely that they actually came across the wastes themselves, always a favoured inroad for West March riders, amply guarded by Naworth, Askerton and Bewcastle. The area's security had not been helped by Elizabeth's penny pinching economic policy, which had allowed all of these fortifications to fall into considerable disrepair.

Therefore the reivers rode unchallenged, though not unobserved. A son of Sir John Heron of Chipchase, keeper of Tynedale, had seen the Scots and knowing only too well what the passage of so many horsemen threatened, had carried the alarm to his parent. Swift, decisive action would have meant that the Scots could be intercepted before they had advanced far enough to do any real damage. In this instance, however, the keeper seemed reluctant to take any positive action and only the mixed threats and entreaties of his brother-in-law, Edward Shaftoe, finally forced Heron to act and muster a body of English horse. Once mustered the riders were not permitted to advance and it was thus that the Scots were able to strike, unhindered, at Haydon Bridge.

For the townspeople there was no succour to be had, their supposed protector remained impotent, nearby Langley Castle was also virtually derelict and apparently unmanned. Rallying bravely the inhabitants grappled and fought with the invaders, leaving a few heads broken on both sides, whilst the town itself was thoroughly ransacked and pillaged with several of the houses set on fire.

Despite the almost cavalier image legend and ballad have bestowed upon Kinmont Willie and his kin there was scant heroism actually attached to their actions. Border raids were aimed simply to loot, and almost anything could fall into that category, though sheep, cattle and horses were the most obvious targets, any valuables and even domestic utensils could be added to the haul. There are instances of clothing, linen, including shrouds and on at least one occasion, several doorframes being included. The reivers, commoner or gentleman, would cheerfully, burn, maim, mutilate and murder to gain these often paltry rewards, and it was only the fear of incurring a blood feud that often prevented purely wanton killing.

In this instance the apparent lack of resistance prompted the Scots into folly which they compounded by dividing their forces, half of which would immediately return by the route they had come, whilst half would strike west and continue their depredations in that March.

The former party found, to their cost, that a number of the English, exasperated by Heron's inactivity, had broken away from his restraining clutches and now pursued the Scots, making seven of their number captive and recovering above a score of lifted beasts.

The other band fell foul of vigilant Cumbrians and were energetically chased back to the border, leaving some of their number slain and much of their booty in the rout.

Thus ended the raid of Haydon Bridge, which was typical of the larger type of foray, though Sir John Heron did not escape criticism for his inaction which, though it may appear incomprehensible to us, was thought only too common at the time. As it was suggested, Sir John appears to have been very well disposed toward the Liddlesdale men and indeed such 'arrangements' were numerous. National duties and responsibilities being often subject to the web of border ties and loyalties, which seldom acknowledged any master other than expediency and the demands of clan kinship and honour.

Chapter Seven

COVENANTERS, KING AND PARLIAMENT

Throughout the Middle Ages the heavily armoured and mounted knight had been the dominating force in warfare. Battles were conventionally decided by the shock of the charge, against which the mass of untrained feudal levies were helpless. As a dominant factor in warfare the heavy cavalryman had had a surprisingly long innings, despite the challenge of the longbow. Latterly however, the infantryman had begun to come into his own. Disciplined bodies of pikemen, advancing in tightly massed formation, such as the redoubtable Swiss mercenaries, proved too much for the feudal host.

By the seventeenth century however, it was common practice to intersperse bodies of musketeers with pikemen for mutual protection. This meant that many infantry battles were decided by 'push of pike' as

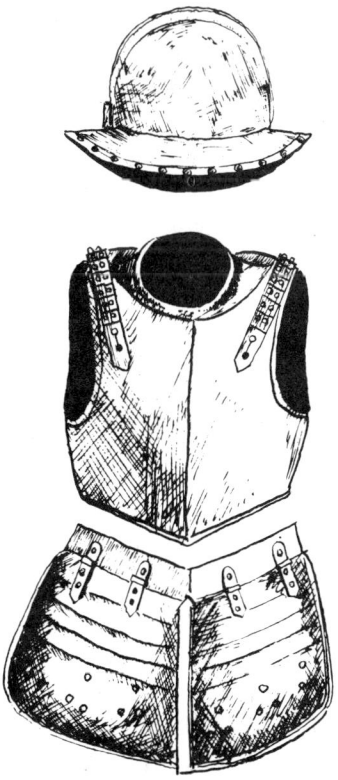

Armour of New
Model Army
pikeman c. 1650.

the cavalry arm had suffered a definite eclipse. If the horse were now unable to effect a successful head on charge they must find some alternative tactic. An early remedy was the 'caracole', which involved a complex manoeuvre designed to permit continuous, close-quarters volley-fire with pistol or carbine. This had severe limitations but it was not until the time of the Thirty Years War that the Swede, Gustavus Adolphus, had developed a solution to the cavalryman's quandry. Now the concept of shock action was reinstated, though the cavalry still used their firearms in a single preliminary volley prior to pressing home the attack with the sword.

Infantry were armed with the pike and the musket. The former varied from twelve to eighteen feet in length and comprised of an ash shaft surmounted by a steel point. The pike was a weapon for the heavier built members of the regiment, who were further encumbered by their protective armour, which generally included a combed helmet, gorget, (to protect the neck), breast and back plates, tassets, (for thigh protection).

Musketeers were more likely to sport wide-brimmed felt hats, and normally did not wear armour. Their principal weapon was the cumbersome matchlock musket. This smooth-bored weapon, which had to be supported on a stick, was primitive in the extreme, slow firing and vulnerable to damp. The range was limited to within one hundred yards at best and accuracy was almost non-existent. Firing was only really effective in massed volleys and these provided the dense clouds of filthy smoke, destined to obscure battlefields until the introduction of the smokeless cartridge, which did not appear until well into the nineteenth century. Both musketeers and pikemen carried short swords or hangers and officers sported a short spear or partisan. The halberd, by no means yet extinct, was retained for sergeants.

A well equipped horseman would boast a carbine and a brace of pistols. These would have either wheel-lock or an early flintlock mechanism, both of which were a vast improvement upon the old matchlock, though considerably more expensive. Swords were invariably carried, though these too varied, from the polished rapiers of the gentlemen and officers to the common broadsword of the lowly trooper. Full armour was now almost extinct though the horseman still wore breast and back plates and the distinctive 'lobster pot' style of helmet. As time progressed however, even this limited amount of armour fell into disuse and was generally abandoned in favour of the buff leather coat, which afforded far greater ease of movement. Such coats however, were again not cheap and a decent one could cost up to ten pounds, a princely sum for that period. The cavalry tended to adopt a sporting, if somewhat amateurish attitude to the war, especially when

Civil War
cavalryman's
armour, helmet
and gauntlet.

led by gentlemen who had learnt their horsemanship on the hunting field and tended to approach a battlefield in like manner. Even if a charge were successful, the advantage was often squandered by the reckless lack of discipline shown by the horse. Such conduct was often fatal. Discipline was not promoted by the disparity of dress, though companies and some regiments were encouraged to standardise, the Whitecoats being a prime example.

Recruitment into armies was, at least in theory, by enlistment but much depended on the local prestige of the officer in question. A seventeenth century landlord, in any country area, could compel his tenants to enlist without a great deal of difficulty and the motivation of many volunteers is open to debate. Needless to say, many men were also pressed into service, and even prisoners of war could be used to bolster the ranks of their captors. Inevitably the desertion rate was high and even the threat of hanging as an accepted punishment did not prove a very effective deterrent.

Stone walls, as a mode of defence, were long since made redundant by the continuing development of artillery. Nevertheless the Civil War abounds with sieges in which apparently outdated city walls and medieval castles held out for long periods even against heavy battering from the guns. Many defenders, appreciating only too well the

135

vulnerable nature of their positions, constructed earthworks outside the original enceinte, which served the dual purpose of both keeping the siege guns at a distance and also providing a more up to date defensive system. Coupled with this the widespread nature of the campaigning made the formation, concentration, and above all, transportation of cumbersome siege artillery difficult in the extreme.

The causes of the English Civil War were numerous and longstanding. Long before Charles came to the throne relations between his autocratic parent James I and his Parliament were far from cordial. James was wanton in his use of regal power, lacking the tact and subtlety of his predecessor, and his actions sowed the seed of his son's destruction.

James did have some good influence on the state of the borders however. As ruler of England and Scotland he was now fully able to check the lawlessness of the 'riding' clans. Ruthlessly but effectively, law and order were established on the borderline, deportation and the rope paved the way for the rule of law. However savage and questionable to modern eyes his chosen methods may have been, James' policy was at least effective and from 1603 folk in the border counties could sleep easier in their beds than they had done for generations past.

Charles I succeeded, upon his father's demise in 1625, but promptly fell under the insidious influence of his father's last favourite George Villiers, Duke of Buckingham, whose conduct only served to exacerbate the rising tension between the monarch and Parliament. Only Buckingham's assassination in 1629 saved the immediate situation. After dissolving Parliament in the same year, Charles embarked upon eleven years of personal rule, where a lethal compound of ignorance, ineptitude and shortage of cash gave birth to one disaster after another. His foreign policy was catastrophic and his policy at home clouded by arrogance and short-sightedness. Charles was totally out of touch with the realities of general opinion in his kingdom. Many people were deeply suspicious and hateful of anything that smacked of popery, especially Charles' Catholic Queen Henrietta Maria, and the anti-Calvinist conviction of Archbishop Laud. the rapidly deteriorating situation was aggravated still further by Charles' efforts to raise money, including the notorious tax known as 'Ship money' — none of which served to bolster his popularity.

Charles was to fare even worse in his dealings with Scotland. Here anti-popery was maintained at a fanatical level and accompanied by a fervently anti-episcopalian attitude which led Charles fatally to interfere. His blundering attempts so outraged the Scots that, in 1638, they drew up the famous National Covenant soon to be backed up by a

Covenanting Army which coerced Charles into concluding the treaty of Berwick. Both sides were equally cynical of the lasting value of this particular truce and Charles was soon attempting to raise an army. This ramshackle force suffered a humiliating debacle at Newburn which meant that Northumberland was once again host to warring armies of English and Scots. Throughout the Civil War period few areas gave greater support to the Royalist cause than the North, which remained loyal to the king throughout the course of his ill-fated clash with Parliament.

The extent of this support was due, in no small measure, to the efforts of William Cavendish, Marquis of Newcastle. Cavendish came from an old Northumbrian family and was a man of considerable wealth, just as well perhaps, as he had spent twenty thousand pounds upon a single entertainment for the King in 1633. In the opening stages of the war he had rallied the North to the King and supported by his famous regiment of Whitecoats, raised at his own expense, he had defeated Sir Thomas Fairfax at Atherton Moor and thus denied Parliament any hold in the north beyond Hull.

Newburn, 1640.

Northumberland had experienced a taste of Civil War as early as the Second Bishops War in 1640 which culminated in the encounter known as the battle of Newburn or perhaps more aptly as 'the Rout of Newburn Ford'. In August of that year the army of the Solemn League and Covenant had crossed the border with twenty thousand foot and two thousand five hundred horse, led by Sir Alexander Leslie of Balgonie, a redoubtable soldier who had served under Adolphus and benefited considerably from his military genius. Consequently the Scots army was drilled and equipped in the most up to date manner.

Once across the Tweed the Scots army progressed by way of Wooler, Eglingham and Netherwitton, not stopping till they reached the banks of the Tyne. The crossing closest to Newcastle was at Newburn, where the river was fordable in two places. Taking up a position that overlooked these crossings the Scots found themselves confronted by an English force gathered on the south bank at Stella Haugh, and obviously intent upon opposing any attempt to cross.

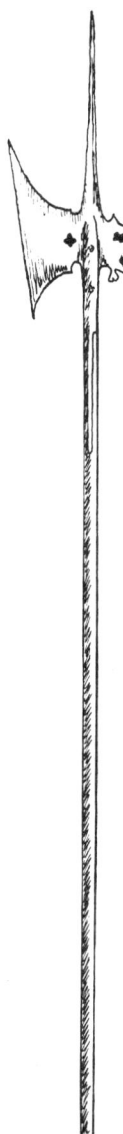

17th Century Halberd.

The English force comprised three thousand five hundred musketeers and two thousand five hundred horse. Their position was consolidated by the hurried erection of two redoubts to cover each of the crossings. In these were placed men of the garrison brought from Newcastle. As dusk fell on the 27th a Scots officer attempted to water his horse in the river, an act of flagrant bravado, which cost him his life

as he was instantly shot from the saddle by an indignant musketeer.

Leslie made good use of the darkness. He mounted a cannon in the tower of Newburn church and had nine more dragged down to the river bank and so positioned as to cover the English redoubts completely. Musketeers were also moved up so that the entire length of the English position could be swept with fire. The cannonade began at dawn on the 28th, the excellent vantage of the higher ground enabled the Scots gunners to make life most uncomfortable for the English in the redoubts.

Under the ample cover of this withering fire a small force of Scottish lifeguards under Major Ballantyne were able to force their way across the river.

Stirrings of panic rippled through the English lines and Lord Conway, the officer commanding, attempting to avoid a rout, ordered the retreat to be sounded. The redoubts were evacuated, thus removing the last obstacle and allowing the bulk of the Scots army to enter the water. The main body of the English were pulled back, and the Scots were ploughing through the shallows, when a small body of horsemen, with typical cavalier elan, charged with reckless gallantry, into the mass of Scots infantry, which though temporarily discomfited, could never be halted by so few. With the failure of this last desperate bid, morale amongst the English collapsed completely and the retreat dissolved into a rout.

Although casualties were light on both sides, the English were so demoralised that Lord Strafford decided to abandon Newcastle, and with it his supplies and munitions to retreat south. Though Strafford was to pay for this desertion with his head, nothing could now prevent the Scots from marching into Newcastle in triumph. Their presence was not as universally abhorrent as might be imagined. The mercantile classes in Newcastle were far less certain in their loyalties than their contemporaries of the county gentry. Sir John Marley, the King's most avid supporter, deemed it wise to flee the city and his successor, Mayor Bewick, was prepared to welcome the Scots.

Leslie was well aware of the strategic importance of Newcastle, both as a centre for exporting coal and as a landing point for any men and/or arms coming in from the continent.

17th Century pikeman's sword.

Whatever enthusiasm some may have felt when the Scots arrived soon evaporated once the Covenanters showed little inclination to leave. The final departure did not occur until 1641 and their stay had cost the city two hundred pounds per day.

Siege of Newcastle, 1644.

By 1643 the whole country was embroiled in Civil War, which had reached virtual deadlock. In order to regain the initiative, Parliament concluded an alliance with Scotland, whereby the Covenanters would commit an army to the war in England on Parliament's behalf.

On the 15th January, 1644 another Scots army, again some twenty thousand strong, crossed the Tweed. Leslie, 'the little old crooked soldier', now made Earl of Leven, was once more in command. There was, in the Scottish ranks, a trooper named Lithgow, a dour, humourless man much given to puritanical sanctimonies, who nevertheless kept a detailed and diligent diary of the ensuing campaign. It is from him that we learn of many of the details of the subsequent siege of Newcastle. Despite the weather, it was a "dismal snowie season," the Scots advanced rapidly through Alnwick and Morpeth. Doubtless Leslie expected Newcastle to fall as easily as it had in 1640. Now, however the situation was entirely different. The Marquis of Newcastle had gathered a sizeable force, including his redoubtable Whitecoats for the defence of the city and had manned and repaired the walls accordingly.

As a further impediment the defenders had erected a pallisaded earthwork with corner bastions known as the Shieldfield fort, some distance from the walls. This contained three hundred defenders and several attempts by the Scots at storming were easily repulsed. All the various houses, barns and outbuildings immediately beyond the perimeter of the walls were burnt to the ground to give the defenders a clear field of fire and also to deprive the attackers of shelter.

With such formidable obstacles before him Leven felt that continued dalliance would be folly and consequently prepared to move his army southward, leaving a mere six regiments of foot and some cavalry under General Lumsdale to cover the city. Cavendish was not prepared for the Scots to escape so lightly, and marshalling his own force, he set off to shadow the southward march. The continued defence of the city was entrusted to Sir John Marley, who now had only one thousand seven hundred defenders at his disposal. Roughly eight hundred of these were drawn from the trained band, the rest comprising 'volunteers, prest-men, coliers, keilmen and poor tradesmen!'

On the 2nd July a bloody and decisive battle was fought at Marston Moor which settled the ultimate fate of Newcastle as surely as if it had been fought outside the city walls. Leven's army fought in the battle, though with something less than distinction, and it was Cromwell's cavalry who decided the day. On the Royalist side none fought harder than the Whitecoats who refused to budge even when the rest of the line disintegrated. Of the thousand who took the field barely thirty survived.

'They would take no quarter, but by mere valour for one whole hour kept the troops of horse from entering amongst them at near push of pike; when the horse did enter they would have no quarter but fought it out till there was not thirty of them living; whose hope it was to be beaten down upon the ground as the troopers came near them, though they could not rise for their wounds, yet were so desperate as to get either pike or sword or a piece of them, and to gore the troopers horses as they came over them or passed them by . . .'

York surrendered within the week and Royalist supremacy in the north was banished forever, Cavendish himself fled to the continent. The Royalist grip could never be finally shattered till Newcastle fell. The bulk of London's coal came from the Tyne and as the saying went 'No hope of yet taking Newcastle by storm and no coals this winter'. Recovering his aplomb after his army's poor performance at Marston Moor, Leven prepared for a return to the north to deal with the situation at Newcastle. Meanwhile, in London coal prices continued to rocket.

A second Scots army of ten thousand men under the Earl of Callender had been dispatched to England as reinforcements.

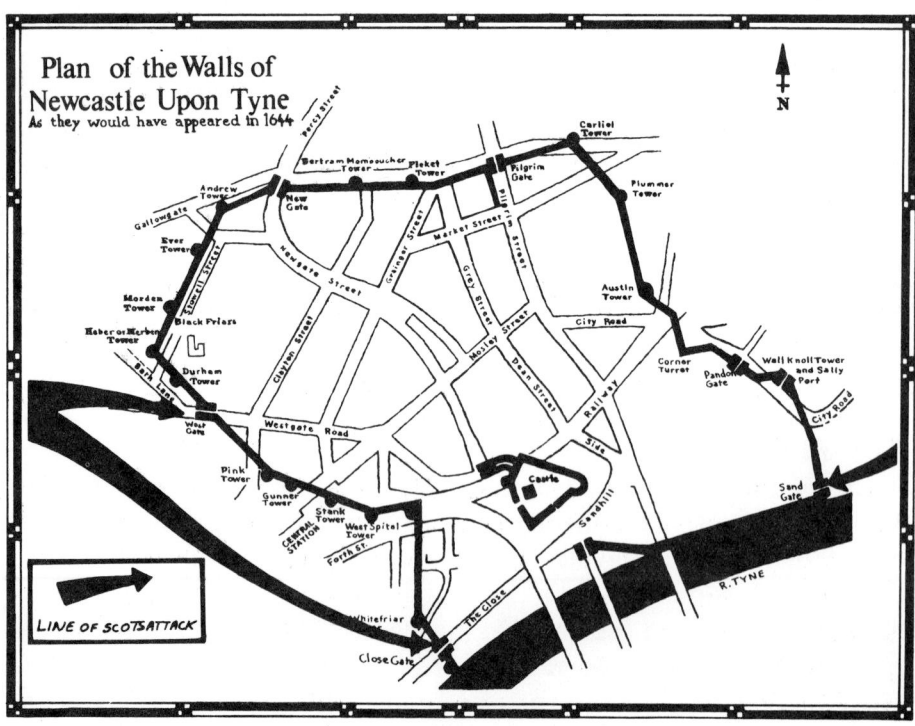

Callender made no attempt to invest Newcastle but was content to take Lumley Castle, Stockton Castle and Hartlepool. Once he had heard of the tale of York however, the Scot prepared to retrace his steps and make some attempt upon the Newcastle defences.

As his forces approached Gateshead a band of Royalists entrenched upon the Windmill Hills were able to halt the vanguard. But once the main body came up a full scale assault on the makeshift defences soon had the royalists scurrying back across the Old Tyne Bridge. Having thus cleared the south bank, Callender had his guns ranged along the riverside and commenced bombarding the city. By way of a response Marley caused the Old Half Moon battery to be repaired and strengthened, from whence soon came a brisk reply to the Scots cannonade.

Presently, this already sizeable force was joined by the remainder of the Scots army, bringing the number of besiegers up to nearly thirty thousand. Several bridges of boats were flung across the river and the encirclement of the city was completed, the siege had begun.

From the outset the position of the defenders was hopeless, the odds, were at best unfortunate, and there was no hope whatsoever of relief. Still, however, they continued to man the walls and repeated calls for surrender, backed up by generous terms, were ignored. Lithgow's impatience with the town's defenders was tempered by a grudging respect for their persistence.

The walls, originally begun in the reign of Edward I, were still a formidable obstacle, even as late as 1644 though artillery had long banished the invincibility of medieval fortifications and Newcastle's walls, unlike those at Berwick, had not been rebuilt with bombardment in mind. The average height was around twelve foot, with an eight foot thickness.

The enceinte was fronted by a ditch twenty two yards wide, six to eight feet deep. The open area between wall and ditch known as a berm, and kept clear to prevent the wall slipping, seems to have been dispensed with at Newcastle. This at least had one advantage in that it made the use of scaling ladders all the more difficult. The gateways were all strongly fortified and the curtain walls between commanded by a series of strong towers. The circumference of the walls is given as two miles, two hundred and thirty nine yards. The towers were generally rectangular on the inner side but rounded on the external face, the circular form being stronger and more resistant to attempts at mining. Of the gates, Newgate and Westgate were the most important; Leland described the latter as a 'Mightye strong thinge'.

The area enclosed by the walls is nowadays almost impossible to determine. On the western side the walls began with the Riverside tower adjacent the Close Gate. A short length of curtain wall was broken by the Whitefriar Tower then the walls ran northward to the Neville Tower, before striking out in a north-westerly direction to reach the West Gate. There were four towers on this stretch — none of which has survived. The section of the walls running parallel to Stowell Street, then past St. Andrews to the New Gate is by far the best preserved, though unfortunately both gateways have been demolished. From the New Gate the curtain ran eastward along Blackett Street to the Pilgrim Gate and then to the Carliol Tower. Turning south we come to the Plumner Tower which survives, the Austin Tower, which does not, and the corner turret, also surviving. Now we pass by the Pandon Gate to the Wall Knoll Tower, the Sallyport and lastly, across City Road to the Sand Gate. A section of wall without towers ran along the river bank. That section of walls which remains intact, beginning from the Durham Tower, adjacent to Bath Lane, and running through the Heber, Morden and Ever Towers, gives a good impression of how the walls should appear. Nevertheless, it would require a formidable imagination to envisage the city and walls as the Scots saw them in 1644. No trace remains of the stout little Shieldfield fort, which did such sterling work in resisting the Scots.

The besiegers were growing impatient with the repeated refusal to surrender and began to press local miners from Benwell and Elswick into service as sappers to undermine the walls. Once galleries beneath the masonry had been dug out mines could be placed and exploded at will. Shortly the Scots were able to plant mines at the Sand Gate and Whitefriars.

The progress of the siege, or rather lack of progress, was watched with growing apprehension in the coal starved capital. Now that winter was approaching supplies of coal were becoming essential. Londoners were further confused by the activities of propagandists from both sides, some would claim that the fall of Newcastle was imminent, others would quote fictitious numbers of Scots slain in futile assaults.

Leven was also persevering with pamphlets, quantities of which were daily flung over the walls. Signing himself rather unimaginatively as a 'well-wisher', the Scot entreated the citizens no longer to trust Sir John Marley and to abandon their futile defence. This campaign was without noticeable effect and Leven decided upon a change of tactics. As a show of strength his artillery concentrated a bombardment upon the section of wall around St. Andrews which was demolished completely. This proved equally unproductive, as by the time the smoke had cleared, the industrious defenders had made good the damage with barricades and continued in their defence.

Four days later, on 3rd October, a sally by the defenders found two

Storming the walls of Newcastle.

of the Scottish mines which were promptly drowned i.e. by flooding galleries. The next day saw a further sally and another device was drowned. This was a considerable boost to the defenders morale and the church bells were heard ringing throughout the night. The austere Lithgow found this celebrating 'insolent'.

The Scots themselves had little cause for rejoicing, the siege was no nearer a conclusion and the news from home was far from encouraging. In the highlands, the redoubtable Montrose had unfurled King Charles' banner and had easily dispersed several Covenanter armies sent against him. Callender's forces were to be withdrawn to help fight Montrose but, at the last minute, Argyll decided to deal with the rebels with the forces he had at hand, unwisely as it transpired, but it meant no slackening of the pressure on Newcastle.

On the 14th October Leven sent a final demand for the surrender of the city. This offer was not rejected outright, and a further suggestion that commissioners from both sides should meet to discuss terms was accepted. A meeting was arranged but soon broke up in disorder, each side alleging that the other was unreasonable. This near-farcical incident meant that any hope for a peaceful end to the siege had vanished. The Scots prepared to storm the city.

Knowing that a major attack was imminent Marley gave orders for the abandonment of the Shieldfield fort — the walls were too thinly manned already to release men for guarding outworks. As the defenders withdrew they fired the pallisade and withdrew into the city under the cover of the smoke.

On the morning of 19th October the Scots prepared for the final attack. The officers threw dice to determine who should lead which section of the attack. The mines at Whitefriars and Sandgate were sprung and other breaches opened by the guns at Westgate and Closegate. As the smoke from the bombardment billowed amongst the crashing masonry, the Scots infantry advanced to the attack and flung themselves upon the breaches. Others, with scaling ladders, fell upon sections of the curtain. Everywhere the attackers met fierce opposition and entry at the breaches was hotly contended. Eventually, the weight of numbers began to tell and the Scots were able to push their way into the city, and the battle for the streets began. Scaling parties finally managed to gain a foothold along the parapets and soon overran several sections of wall, though defenders holed up in the towers, continued to resist. The Scots were now pouring through the breaches, but the passage had cost them dear, amongst the slain was Colonel Home, a notably courageous officer.

Woe to that breach beside Black Bessies Towre,
Woe to itself that bloudy butchering bower!
Where valiant Home, that stern Bellona's blade,
And brave commander fell: For there he stay'd
arraigned by death.

The defenders fell back, street by street, contesting every yard by push of pike. The stiffness of the fight impressed even the dour Lithgow:—

'The thousand of musket balls flying from other faces like to the droving haylestones from septentrian blast; the clangour and carving of naked unsheathed swords; the pushing of broughing pikes crying for blood: the carkasses of men lying like dead dogs upon the groaning street.'

Gradually the tide of resistance began to ebb and the surviving defenders laid down their arms, so that within two hours of the mines being sprung the Scots had complete possession of the town. They had paid dearly for it leaving nearly one thousand dead in the breaches and the bloody streets beyond. The defenders seem to have escaped serious loss, though the town was given over to sack for twenty four hours, as custom permitted after a storming. Sir John Marley and some fellow diehards had retreated into the castle itself, built in the reign of Henry II, but still a formidable bastion. At first Marley continued in token defiance though soon he was asking for terms and finally, when these were not forthcoming, accepted unconditional surrender.

Marley was soon back in the castle, this time in the dungeons, whilst the Scots celebrated their triumph with a thanksgiving service in St. Nicholas Church. One of Leven's earliest threats had apparently been a promise to demolish the spire of St. Nicholas by bombardment. Marley had replied by cramming the church with Scots prisoners and then inviting Leven to proceed.

Leven had now promised the execution of Sir John, but the Mayor replied to this by escaping from custody, eventually succeeding in making good his escape to the continent. There he joined the legions of other exiled Royalists, returning with them at the Restoration when he was reinstated as Mayor of Newcastle and also elected as an MP for the city, in which capacity he served until his death.

The relief in the capital was so profound that a day of public thanksgiving was proclaimed for November 5th, with the coal trade able to be resumed the city was saved from freezing. The siege of Newcastle had lasted for three months and though there was never really any point to the continued resistance the defenders had proved themselves worthy of the motto 'Fortiter Defendit Triumphans,' (she bravely and triumphantly defends).

The speed of urban development in the last three centuries has precluded the possibility of our being able to identify the scenes of the action at the time of the storming. We can say that as the Scots effected breaches at Whitefriars, Close Gate and Sandgate, their advance into the city would come via the Close and Sandhill. The final breach at West Gate would bring them down Westgate Road. In all probability the defenders would be gradually pushed down toward the Bigg Market, where the final capitulation would take place.

Chapter Eight

JACOBITES AND RIOTERS

Derwentwater's Rebellion, 1715.

> Lord Derwentwater to Forster said
> Thou had ruin'd the cause, and all betray'd
> For thou didst vow to stand our friend
> But thou hast prov'd traitor in the end.
> Thou brought us from our own country;
> We left our homes, and came with thee,
> But thou art a rogue and a traitor both,
> And hast broke thy honour and thy oath.

> James Hogg: *The Jacobite relics of Scotland being the song, airs and legend of the adherents to the House of Stuart.*

The siege and storming of Newcastle was the final major campaign in Northumberland's battle-scarred history. Saxon and Dane were long forgot, the two kingdoms united and even the wild dark border riders subdued.

When the carnage of the Civil War was finally over, it was followed by the austerity of the Commonwealth and then, in 1660, by the Restoration of the monarchy. Charles II was too canny to tread his father's fatal footsteps and had no desire 'to be off on his travels' again. His catholic brother, James II, who succeeded him, was considerably less prudent and after three years on the throne was sent packing in favour of his Dutch son-in-law, William of Orange.

This final displacement of the Stuart kings gave birth to the most romanticised of all lost causes, the white cockade; the Jacobites. Few have inspired so many brave but foolish men to so much reckless and fatal gallantry, and of all of these perhaps none was so gallant or so foolish as the last Earl of Derwentwater. Though the Stuarts would never again enjoy the measure of armed support given to Charles I during the Civil War, a hardcore of catholic northern gentry still longed for a return to the old days before the 'Glorious Revolution' of 1688. The image of these Northumbrian Jacobites has been indelibly linked to that of the fictional inhabitants of Osbaldistone Hall, hard-riding, hard-drinking, fanatically conservative and not over-burdened with grey matter. True or otherwise the Jacobites, as they were to discover, were very much of a minority even amongst their own classes.

The manor of Dilston had belonged to a Norman Knight, William Fitz Aluric during the reign of Henry I. The fief passed first to the Tynedales and then, in the fifteenth century, to the Radcliffe family. At this time the bulk of their estates lay in Cumberland, but Sir Cuthbert moved the family seat into Northumberland and the Radcliffes swiftly climbed to prominence in the county. In 1545 Sir George Radcliffe became High Sheriff and Lord Warden of the East Marches. As staunch catholics and Royalists they were out during the course of the Civil War, and lost their estates in consequence. The Restoration of the monarchy saw the full restoration of their estates and the grateful Charles II created a Radcliffe 1st Earl of Derwentwater.

The third and last earl was born James Radcliffe in 1689 and came into the title in 1705. Inevitably he was well schooled in the family tradition, a fatal alliance that was cemented by schooling at the exiled Stuart court of St. Germain. The Radcliffes had never made any secret of their loyalties and no sooner had the banner of the White Cockade been raised in Scotland at the outset of the '15 than a warrant was immediately issued for the arrest of the Earl of Derwentwater.

James avoided incarceration by a swift retirement into hiding, keeping a low profile paid dividends and the Earl avoided capture throughout the summer of 1715. Despite the hounds that were ever at his heels he had still not formally committed himself to the Stuart cause. Derwentwater was not such a fool that he did not hesitate to pledge himself, his life and fortune, to so hazardous a venture. To gamble so much on such an uncertain throw can hardly have appealed, and even the strong call of family loyalties and tradition could not move him to the final, irretrievable step. In this however, malicious fate had a powerful and damming ally in the person of the Countess herself, an utterly fanatical Jacobite. It was her scorn and her entreaties that ultimately drove her wavering husband to finally declare for the Pretender, a course that would lead him inexorably towards the scaffold.

It was in October that the last Earl of Derwentwater rode out from Dilston at the head of a small body of friends and retainers. His was not a lone decision, several other groups of Northumbrian Jacobites were already out and James' little force joined up with a larger body, led by his cousin Tom Forster, at Greenrigg near Hexham.

Together, the cousins rode with their joint forces toward Morpeth, where a general muster of the rebels was to be held. The muster however, did not show a very convincing picture, as the total Jacobite 'army' numbered less than three hundred. This unhappy discovery was further clouded by a wrangle over who should now assume overall command. The two principal candidates were Forster and Derwentwater and of these, the former seemed, at least on paper, to be the most likely choice; ten years the senior, an MP and lastly and most telling, a protestant. Though Derwentwater was by far the most popular it was felt that his ardent catholicism might deter Anglicans from joining the rebellion, whereas a protestant commander would present no such obstacle. In the end it was Forster that was chosen and, all in all, a worse leader would have been hard to find.

The rebels were at least unanimous upon their prime objective, Newcastle, the securing of which would depend on striking whilst they still had the initiative. Instead of exploiting this slender advantage however, Forster was content to let it slip away, whilst he embarked on a futile nine day horseback tour of the country, dragging his bewildered followers behind him. Supposedly aimed at boosting their recruitment levels the Jacobites' march led them through Rothbury and down the length of the Coquet to Warkworth, where 'James III' was solemnly proclaimed King of England. From there, the road led back to Morpeth their only prize being a captive local blacksmith kidnapped en route.

This time Newcastle began to look a long, long way away, for the city, which had held out so long and so hard for Charles I, was now swift to scorn his descendant. The time that the rebels had so wantonly squandered had been put to much better use by the Tyneside magistrates. All suspected Jacobites had been rounded up and gaoled, the city's ancient defences were once again overhauled and made ready, the militia and the trained bands mustered. Whig gentlemen and their tenants flocked to the Hanoverian standard, and by 9th October a body of regular troops had arrived at Newcastle. The magistrates now felt that they had cause to be reasonably confident.

'General' Tom Forster was now a long way less than confident and rather than advance on Newcastle decided to retire to Hexham, where the Jacobite leader and his tiny army kicked their heels in mounting frustration and despair. So far the only military success that the rebels could boast was the storming of Holy Island castle by a company under the command of Lancelot Errington. Their occupation only lasted for a day and the whole affair assumed almost comic proportions, though it is unlikely the Jacobites themselves, now totally committed to a course that seemed increasingly hopeless, appreciated this aspect of the situation.

Whilst the rebels hesitated in the mire of their own indecision, the Government forces were preparing to act and seize the initiative. On 18th October, General George Carpenter led Cobhams, Molesworth's and Churchill's regiments into Newcastle, his orders were both simple and explicit, he was charged to:—

'Go in pursuit of the rebels whithersoever they went'.

In pursuance of the order the General prepared for a march upon the rebels, now gathered despondently at Hexham.

Though their fate now seemed almost sealed, the Jacobites were yet to be granted one last reprieve, in the unexpected form of a summons to join forces with a body of lowland Scots, who, having also espoused the cause of the white cockade, had descended on Rothbury. The reunion served to revive the flagging hopes of Forster and Derwentwater as the two forces, roughly equal in size, swelled the streets and taverns of the small market town, carousing raucously in the Three Half Moons and the Old Black Bull.

After the brandy fumes had cleared the Jacobites moved on to Wooler but their swollen ranks did not deter General Carpenter from continuing his offensive preparations. Again the rebels took to the road marching north, away from their dogged adversary, to Kelso where their numbers were again increased by the arrival of McIntosh's Highlanders. Though very welcome the new arrivals posed some fresh difficulties over who was now to assume overall command, and again the choice fell upon the incompetent Forster, despite the almost universal dislike he had managed to inspire among his peers.

Swaggering under the influence of his new command, the rebel general led his much travelled army back along the road to England. The new plan was that the Jacobites should march through Cumberland and into Lancashire where it was hoped that some local support might be forthcoming. From the day they re-crossed the border on November 1st the rebels moved inexorably toward their final nemesis at Preston, where the joint forces of Generals Wills and Carpenter finally caught up with them.

Forster's deplorable handling of the situation came to a fitting end with a shameful and catastrophic surrender to the government forces investing the town. On November 14th some sixteen hundred Jacobites laid down their arms and marched into captivity. The haul included Forster himself, Derwentwater and seventy-five other Northumbrian gentry.

Some were summarily executed in Lancashire, but the majority were taken to London and herded into the city's gaols. Forster found

Jacobites at bay — an end to the rebellion.

himself in Newgate, from where he managed to escape and thus cheated the block of a most deserving victim.

Derwentwater himself was less fortunate and as befitted his rank he was tried before the bar of the House of Lords, in January, 1716. In spite of a personal defence conducted with considerable dignity and some skill, the verdict was never really in doubt and the last Earl of Derwentwater went bravely to the block on 24th February. Thus he put. the final tragic seal on a career distinguished by that brand of, almost quixotic, gallantry that so characterised the doomed adherents of the House of Stuart.

James' younger brother Charles Radcliffe was also out in the rebellion, and was also condemned to death, but managed to slip the bands of justice and escape to France. His brother's fate seems to have taught Charles Radcliffe very little, for he was out again thirty years later in the '45 and was again caught and condemned, but this time he failed to cheat the executioner.

The Crookham Affray, 1678.

Of all the affairs and encounterings that form the pages of the border chronicles, some like Flodden or Otterburn stand out as the biggest and the bloodiest. The 'affray' at Crookham, however, must rank as one of the least, in terms of human casualties.

As in most of Northumberland's major clashes the combatants were English and Scots, though for once it was not a difference of nationality that led to the fight, but more a matter of religious conviction.

Immediately following the restoration of the Stuart monarchy in the 1670's and 1680's Northumberland became the backdrop for a bitter, uncompromising and increasingly violent struggle, that was being enacted north of the border. Released from the dour astringencies of the Commonwealth the Episcopalian church was once again in the ascendant, ousting the austere, bigoted, convenanting ministers from their pulpits and sowing the seeds of bitter discord throughout the Scottish borderland.

Thus it was, that during those troubled years of 1660-1689, the county was to provide an easy and safe refuge for renegade preachers and other fugitives, whose fervent allegiance to the Solemn League and Covenant had made their side of the border too hot to hold them. First a refuge and then a rallying ground, as the number of exiles and the bitterness of the struggle swelled, Northumberland became host to a bevy of secret conventicles and hidden trysts. As this rising tide of dissention grew, it seemed as though the state of open war extant north of the border could once again roll southward over the Tweed, bringing attendant ruin in its merciless train.

At first hesitant and unwilling the Northumbrian justices, good country gentry and Episcopalians all, were eventually stirred toward a policy of repression, aimed at stamping out the impending holocaust before it actually erupted. Inevitably, this hardening attitude lent fuel to an already smouldering fire.

'John Welsh a Phanaticke Preacher, aged betwixt 50 and 60 years, is a thicke short man, within these few years inclined to be fatt . . .'

Thus ran the description of the renegade preacher John Welsh, a gentleman who was distinguished by other qualities than middle age spread. He belonged originally to the Dumfries and Galloway region and had graduated in the singularly uncompromising era of the Commonwealth. He was, infact, a great-grandson of the towering genius of the Scottish Reformation, the redoubtable and vitriolic John Knox himself. Imbued with all of the furious fervour of this distinguished forbear, Welsh was not one to be deterred either by the Restoration or his own, subsequent eviction in 1662/63. His enthusiasm was, if anything, increased by such persecution. Roving and preaching throughout the border he graduated further into that select band that included Semple, Peden, Blackadder and Arnott, the apprehension, of whom was most eagerly sought by the authorities.

One gentleman particularly anxious to lay hands upon the nimble clergyman was William Strother, a Northumbrian J.P. and staunch cavalier. Born in 1625 and active in his late majesty's forces throughout the whole bloody trauma of the Civil Wars, he had seen more recent service against the convenanters in Scotland and had no sympathy whatsoever with the subversive activities of the rebel ministers. Welsh had been seeking regular refuge in Northumberland since 1676, flitting to and fro across the border with apparent importunity. Such liberties had hardened the choleric justices' resolve to — 'spare no pains to take the rebel . . .' The fact that the Scotsman's head carried a price of four hundred pounds upon it can only have served to strengthen this already considerable zeal.

In the high summer of 1678 the Scottish justice Lord Home received word that a band of fugitives, including the 'Phanaticke Preacher' himself, were in hiding on the English side of the Tweed at Learmouth, scarcely three miles south of his own house at the Hirsel. Powerless to act himself, his lordship lost no time in informing his English counterparts of this nest of vipers within their own boundaries.

Such intelligence was not wasted upon William Strother. From his home at Fowberry he swiftly gathered a small but picked band of cavaliers, each related by blood or marriage and seasoned campaigners all. John Strother, brother; John Salkeld of Rock, brother-in-law, sixty-two years of age and as staunch a cavalier as ever cleared steel from leather; Robert Marley, cousin and a son of the famous Sir John, lord mayor and defender of Newcastle.

With this determined company, and a handful of mounted retainers, Strother set out on the road for Learmouth in the small hours of Saturday, September 14th, hoping to fall upon his unsuspecting prey by daybreak. Considering that the convenanters were known to be several in number, and most unlikely to be inclined toward a peaceful surrender, a rope their only likely measure of justice, the English would not enjoy superiority of numbers. No doubt it was the advantage of speed, rather than the temptation of the reward, that deterred the valiant cavaliers from calling upon the aid of a troop of dragoons stationed at Wooler.

The excitement of the chase proved more inspiring than the prize, for the sleepy little hamlet yielded no better catch than one George Hume of Graden, a known convenanter but no great triumph for all that. Doubtless now somewhat disgruntled, the justices jostled their captive back over the fulsome waters of the Tweed and brought him before Lord Home at the Hirsel.

This, in itself, must have been something of an embarrassment to the Scottish peer who, on being informed that the birds had flown, felt obliged to explain that their escape was undoubtedly due to his own indiscretion.

Graden, though a convenanter, was still a gentleman and as such had actually dined at the Hirsel the night before. No doubt the port had passed around the table and liberal measures dispensed to all the guests. Inevitably, this had served to promote the level of conversation, loosening tongues that might otherwise have kept still. Chief amongst these was mine host himself, who was prompted to admonish Graden with the follies of his convictions, a homily concluded with a solemn warning that the English justices would shortly descend upon himself and his friends at Learmouth.

Thus alerted the covenanter wasted no time in taking his leave and making his way, poste haste, back over the border in time to deliver a timely warning to his fellow fugitives. As it happens, none of these was Welsh, but a party of Scots gentry comprising; Thomas Ker of Hayhope, James Pringle, son of the laird of Buckholm, Henry Hall of Haughhead, Alexander Home and lastly one Hector Aird, staunch adherents of the kirk to a man.

By the time the English cavaliers clattered into Learmouth the Scots were long gone except, of course, for poor Graden himself who had decided to snatch a few hours slumber before joining his friends in flight. Now he was back at the Hirsel, though this time the invitation was of a more compelling nature and the atmosphere decidedly less cordial. It was decided that he should be incarcerated in the grim bastion of Home Castle — a formidable and convenient gaol. Though, according to the strict letter of the law, Graden should have been conveyed to Morpeth, located in the county wherein he was apprehended, and from whence appropriate extradition proceedings could be instigated. Doubtless Strother had other things to say to Lord Home, it is perhaps as well that these do not seem to have been recorded.

Though now flushed from their safe house the fugitive Scots were far from dismayed or demoralised and were in fact determined to rescue their saviour Graden, from captivity. They were convinced, rightly, if due course of law were to be observed, that the English would ride south with their prisoner, first to Wooler and then on to gaol at Morpeth. Consequently, they agreed to meet and regroup at the house of a sympathiser at Crookham from whence they could intercept the returning cavaliers and relieve them of their prize. Hunter and hunted had swapped roles.

Whilst dining at Crookham the covenanters were dismayed to hear that Graden was now incarcerated in Home Castle and that Strother's party were fast approaching, though as there was no captive, the proposed rescue attempt had to be hurriedly abandoned. The Scots were now in something of a quandary, should they stay? Should they fight? Should they flee? It seemed to Ker, apparently the natural leader of the band, that their best course was to mount up and seek a quiet way north, one that would get them clear of the approaching justices without provoking an encounter. Regrettably, this plan went slightly astray in that both parties came face to face upon the narrow highway. Glaring at each other like contestants in a western gun duel the horsemen sat indecisive in silent hostility, all no doubt wondering exactly what was going to happen next.

At first it appeared as though common sense might yet prevail. Ker and his party were certainly not spoiling for a fight, nor, it seems were the elder cavaliers. After all it was the preacher Welsh that they really sought and these particular Scots had yet to offend any law of England. All might have ended peacefully had it not been for the younger Englishman, Marley, who, doubtless fired by the history of his father's famed defiance of the covenanters, rode up to Ker demanding of him that he should now surrender.

'Why?' enquired the Scotsman, not unreasonably. What were the charges? Where was the warrant for his arrest?

Unable to produce answers to either of the responses, Marlay instead produced his pistol and shot the covenanter at point blank range, inflicting a mortal wound. Stricken though not yet slain, Ker managed to draw his own weapon and return his adversary's fire. The ball caught Marley squarely between the eyes, spinning him lifeless from the saddle. It would take more than first blood to settle this affair, however, and the calm of the evening was shattered by the rattle of musketry.

With a final, despairing burst of effort the dying Ker urged his mount into a frightened canter, and discharging a second pistol, he cannoned into the ranks of the English party, even managing to draw his sword before finally toppling from the saddle to expire in the dusty roadway. Still however, not before he gasped out a final exhortation to his battling countrymen, now fully engaged in a furious mêlée with the surviving cavaliers.

The flash and roar of flintlocks added chorus to the scrape and clang of tangled blades, men and horses lunged and careered in a deadly confusion that swirled and eddied along the highway. Strother tumbled in the dirt as his riddled mount foundered beneath him, but several of the Scots, including Home and Hall, were left reeling and bloody in their saddles, as the ring of English steel around them parried and thrust in a murderous confusion.

The fight lasted no more than a few savage, incoherent moments before the Scots were through the barrier of men and horses, galloping hard for the north and for safety. It does appear that nearly all of them had been wounded though none save Ker were slain.

O Light of Kindness, Nature mild and good!
O true religious Son! O Nation's lover!
O soul sublimer than these heavens could cover,
O Noble Ker. O patron of Renown!
We groan on Earth, thou wears a heavenly crown!

Thus began and ended the Crookham affray. One cavalier and one covenanter lay dead, each slain by the hand of the other. There was no pursuit from the dazed judiciary and the escaping Scots lived to fight another day. There was a subsequent rumour that young Pringle had died from wounds sustained in the affair, though, in all probability, it does appear that this was a ruse to allay possible fear of capture. Home, certainly was active in later skirmishes and avoided the rope for another three years until he was finally taken, and hanged at the Mercat Cross in Edinburgh.

The encounter was doubtless refought many times around the dining table at Fowberry, but in all it was a pointless affair that the majority of the protaganists would have preferred to have avoided, including one suspects, Strother himself. The incident is well recorded though largely forgotten and the site, needless to add, is not marked on the O.S. map.

Hexham Market Place 'A spectacle that hurt humanity,' 1761.

Quaint old Hexham market — surely all that a country market square should be, flanked on its western side by the eastward face of the Priory looking across to the solid pile of the Moot Hall, which started life in the fourteenth or fifteenth century as a tower house. The most noticeable features of the square are the Temperley Memorial Fountain (1901), and the Shambles, an open colomnaded structure built by Sir Walter Blackett in 1766. It is a tranquil scene, little altered in recent years, save that the western side was originally hemmed in by housing that was demolished in the reign of Victoria.

Five years before the Shambles were built, in 1761, things were noticeably less restful. George III was on the throne and the Hanoverian line seemed well established and secure. The failure of the '45 and the holocaust at Culloden had finally pulverized the Jacobite menace. The dour, Germanic Georges did not enjoy universal popularity, some of the Northern gentry still toasted the king 'over the water'. The King's first minister, the Earl of Bute, was cordially detested, except one assumes, amongst the select ranks of Sir Francis Dashwood's Hellfire Club, in which he was the leading light.

Costly and seemingly endless continental wars had drained England of regular troops, which meant that large bodies of men had to be drafted into the militia. Normally this chore was the responsibility of the local landowners, but this was passed to the magistrates when it was proposed to decide the enlistments by ballot.

The entire scheme proved universally abhorrent and savage riots broke out in several Northumbrian towns where the system was attempted. The disturbances at centres such as Alnwick, Gateshead and Whittingham were so violent that the magistrates' lost their collective nerve and withdrew the ballot.

At Hexham, it was to be different, here the magistrates were determined to do their duty come what may. To help maintain law and order the deputy lieutenant drafted in two regiments of the New Yorkshire Militia from Newcastle. It appears that this was never intended as anything more than a peace-keeping measure, though in the general air of unease and discontent, the arrival of so many Red-coats must have taken on a far more sinister aspect.

The balloting at Hexham was to take place in the Moot Hall on 9th March and in the early morning the newly arrived infantry were formed up around three sides of the square, the bulk of the Moot Hall itself forming a fourth side. The stiff ramrod backed lines of scarlet and white, their fixed bayonets glinting dully in the pallid light of early March, must have seemed almost grotesquely incongruous amid the sombre aged stones of the market square. An ominous note of warning sounded when a proclamation was read urging the honest citizens to keep within doors.

It was just as well, from Corbridge, Slaley, Bywell, Prudhoe, Newburn, Haydon Bridge, Blanchland, Simonburn and Corsenside an army of vociferous protesters, men, women and children, nearly five thousand strong, was soon tramping down the lanes and byways. A shapeless, ragged mass, clad in shabby homespun clothing — a more marked contrast to the silent uniformed, brass-buttoned ranks of the militia could scarcely be imagined.

Undeterred, the magistrates were determined to proceed, refusing several petitions from the crowd, which though affirming their loyalty to King George, refused to submit to the ballot. This obstinacy led to a rapid worsening situation as the crowd became yet more noisy and restless, cudgels, staves and even firearms were openly brandished. The magistrates could now see that the confrontation they had helped to create was slipping out of their control, in a desperate and largely fatuous effort to restore both order, and their crumbling prestige, they caused the Riot Act to be read out.

This particular gesture only served to exacerbate the degree of knife edge tension in the square, nor was this tension confined to the crowd. For nigh on three hours the part-time soldiery had silently borne anger, insult and abuse, their nerves being gradually stretched almost to breaking point by the vast, hostile mob that seemed poised at any moment, to engulf them. What had seemed a simple exercise, nothing more than routine police work, appeared poised to erupt into a full scale war.

Reading the Riot Act had really been the justices' last throw, and its inneffectiveness had robbed them of the initiative which had now passed to the rioters. Sensing the indecision, and growing bolder, a body of protesters suddenly fell upon a detachment of Redcoats. A musket, dropped in the ensuing scuffle, was employed with fatal effect against one of the soldiery and Young Ensign Hart of Darlington received a pistol ball for his pains as he struggled to restore order.

It was then, with a swift certain precision, both terrible and deadly, the ranks of shouldered arms were suddenly presented and levelled. All earlier tumult drowned by the shattering roar of the volley, reverberating around the open square like the veritable clap of doom. Brown Bess, the regnant queen of Europe's battlefields, had brought her lethal trade to Hexham's market.

Once the filthy smoke had cleared, the powder blackened men of the North Yorkshire Militia were able to survey their handiwork, for the square was empty now, save for the heaps of pathetic human bundles, writhing and groaning or still, crumpled sack-like in death and mutilation. Only the blood, flowing freely in great torrents amongst the cobbles, was left to proclaim them remnants of humanity. The butcher's bill for the carnage is put at forty-five dead and over three hundred injured, women and children featured prominently in both groups.

But still the killing had not stopped. Dragoons were presently scouring the countryside for the rioters and their ringleaders. Of those who were arrested two, Peter Patterson and William Elder, were subsequently condemned to death. Though the latter was granted a last minute reprieve the former was made to suffer the full savagery of the law:—

'. . . . You must be drawn to the Place of Execution. When you do come there, you must be hanged by the Neck, but not till you are Dead, for you must be cut down alive; then your Bowels must be taken out and burned before your face; then your Head must be severed from your Body and your Body divided into four Quarters, and these must be at the King's disposal.'

Patterson was, at this time, 74 years of age.
Quaint old Hexham market.

Chapter Nine

WIND, WAVES AND NORTHERN
PIRATES HANDS

'In this year (793) terrible portents appeared in Northumbria and miserably frightened the inhabitants: There were exceptional flashes of lightning, and fiery dragons were seen flying in the air, and soon followed a great famine, and after that in the same year the harrying of the heathen miserably destroyed Gods church in Lindisfarne by rapine and slaughter.'

The holy island of Lindisfarne is steeped in the lifeblood of this region's history and occupies a space in the chronicles of Northumbria out of all proportion to its mere one thousand three hundred and fifty acres, indeed the county has few more romantic or dramatic vistas than the first sight of the castle perched atop its lonely basalt outcrop.

Island or archipelago dependent upon the ebb and flow of the tide Lindisfarne first achieved prominence after 635 when Aidan chose it for the seat of his episcopacy — this was to be the seed of that great flowering of the golden era destined to push back the savage mists of the dark ages and make the island famous for two full centuries.

It was later that the holy shore became host to a more predatory breed of visitor, no gentle, pious monks these but hardened brutal heathens who rowed their awesome square sailed galleys over the forbidding reaches of the North Sea to pounce upon the hapless clerics. Prelate Higbald and his brethren, those who still survived, were forced to flee to the comparative sanctuary of the mainland, the acrid stench of blood and burning timbers still pursuing them across the narrow waters.

This was the kingdom's first bitter taste of the Norseman's fury, it was not to be the last, from now on thane and villager alike would scan the eastern horizon, dreading the first shout of warning, the call to arms as the sinister dragon headed prows of the longships hove menacingly into view. Then it was time for fear.

Though the monks returned to Lindisfarne after the raid of 793 the magic of the place had gone, washed away by the blood of so many of their companions. Now the paramount thought was that one day the sea wolves would return and harry the defenceless monastery again. Though left in peace for over eighty years the island was again pillaged in 875 — the longships were first beached at Tynemouth where the priory was mercilessly harried. Proceeding by flame scarred stages along the coastline the northmen again descended upon Lindisfarne where the broadsword and torch soon found busy employment.

Thrusting the body of St. Cuthbert into a wooden coffin alongside the head of St. Oswald and gathering the bones of Bishops Aidan, Eata, Eadfrid, Ethelwold and others the monks once again sought refuge in flight — this time they did not return, it was not until after the Norman conquest, in 1093, that the priory was reinstated. Whether it was their bitter experiences with the sea raiders or not, later, secular inhabitants of the island were notably less pious and decidedly more materialistic, seeming to have more in common with their Norse persecutors than their ecclesiastical forbears. A seventeenth century description of the islanders comments somewhat sourly on their enthusiastic plundering of those vessels unfortunate enough to be wrecked or driven ashore in nearby waters.

'He told us how the common people ther do pray for shippes which they see in danger, They al sit down upon their knees and hold up their handes, and say very devotely "Lord, send her to us; God, send her to us." "You," said he, "seeing them upon their knees, and their hands joyned, do think that they are praying for your sauvetie, but their myndes are far from that. They pray not to God to sauve you, or send you to the port, but to send you to them by shipwreck, that they may gette the spoil of her.'

Northumbria has a long coastline, full of contrasts, miles of glorious rolling sands vie with gaunt, jutting cliffs and seemingly endless ranks of dunes all facing the indomitable waves of the cold northern sea that has raged and battered throughout the millenia. Sea birds swoop and screech above white capped breakers, a pattern of rock girt islets are scattered like pebbles amidst the timeless seasons of the waves. It is a coast of hardness and of beauty, the chill seems always enough to deter all but the hardiest bathers, shaped but not degraded by the pounding of the centuries, generally free of the worst of man's excesses, for the moment at least, and in parts of almost virgin purity.

Stretched between the floods of Tyne and Tweed Northumbria's coastal strand has seen its fair share of marauders and invaders; it was here that the Norsemen drew first blood, though they were not the earliest if certainly the most predatory of visitors — Saxon Ida and his followers came by ship, as had many previous immigrants. Even after the spate of invasions and sea wolves had died out there were those who found the many coves and inlets along the lonely shore ideal for the movement of 'innocent' or smuggled goods.

As late as 1691 sea-raiders were to be seen off the Northumbrian coast. These latter day rovers were not Norse but French privateers led by the famous brigand Jean Bart whose squadron comprising the *Alcion, Conte, Heureuse, Tigre, Aurore,* and *Railleur* made landfall in Druridge Bay piloted thither by one Chetworth, an English renegade. A raiding party commanded by Count Forbin, friend and confederate of the great privateer himself came ashore in the boats and scaled the sea cliffs to fall upon Druridge village. The buccaneers burnt and pillaged, though the poor, humble fishermen's cottages would provide only meagre pickings. Obviously in the hope of better things the raiders next descended upon Widdrington Castle which was also duly looted, finally they concluded the business of the evening by firing Chibburn Preceptory, an ancient ediface, originally founded by the Knights Hospitaller in the fourteenth century.

The late eighteenth and early nineteenth centuries were the heyday of the smugglers whose activities were far from the romantic image of the legends, theirs was simply a business, nothing more, and often a very lucrative business and incidentally one that could put a rope around the neck of anyone caught in the act. For years the upper reaches of Coquetdale were a base for the distillers of illicit spirits whose activities continued almost uninterrupted despite the best efforts of the excisemen of gaugers, in crude but superbly camouflaged stills that were so cunningly designed and built as to almost form part of the natural topography.

The coastal sanctuary for the smugglers at this time was the village of Bulmer (Boulmer) the most famous of whom was the landlord of the Fishing boat Inn, Isaac Addison. Mine host obviously believed in living up to his daredevil image which, in itself, would certainly benefit the licensed branch of his trade. Evidently a man of some refinement and education as well as having a shrewd head for business he was well able to keep his patrons, including the Duke of Northumberland himself, supplied with a plentiful stock of tall tales, which doubtless grew taller as the evening wore on and the ale flowed more freely.

Despite his cavalier attitude 'Isaac the Smuggler' was no vain boaster, his vessel the *Ides* plied the Northumbrian seaboard well laden with innocent liquor a trade that continued without threat and with heartwarming profit for some years. Inevitably there came a day when luck finally ran out, nemesis in the form of the dreaded excise cutter bore down upon the *Ides* as she ran, fully laden for the safety of Bulmer Harbour.

For all that it was so widespread smuggling was still no petty offence and Isaac with a full crew of two dozen hands was not about to haul his colours without a fight. Soon the sea air was buzzing with lead shot and the crackle of fire as the encounter burgeoned into a full scale sea battle between the 'Ides' and the excise cutter. Throwing on every inch of canvas the smugglers attempted to outpace the cutter in a race along the coast but the gaugers were too close to the scent of triumph to give in so easily and they took off in full cry swapping shots with the *Ides* whenever she came in range.

As darkness was falling the fight still raged with furious intensity, two at least of the smugglers' rounds had found a mark though one of their number lolled lifeless in the gunwhales and another ground his teeth against the agony of a leg shattered by a heavy ball. Convinced now there was little hope of throwing off such a determined pursuit the smugglers used the fast descending cloak of night to mask their retreat. Loading their dead and wounded into the boat, doubtless with as much of their illicit cargo as could be easily carried the faithful *Ides* was left to settle, her sea cocks wide open treating the hovering gaugers to the sight of the evidence quite literally dissappearing into the greater darkness before their eyes.

Then it was every man to the oars as the smugglers pulled for the land, their tired muscles lent extra strength by the sure knowledge that a rope's end would be their certain fate if taken. Fortune smiled upon them once again however and the longboat was carried ashore in Bulmer harbour long before the excise cutter slid through the entrance. When the gaugers finally weighed anchor and marched upon the quiet hamlet there was, inevitably, no sign of their quarry, even the getaway boat had vanished, Isaac having had the foresight to strip the boat down and stash its members at a cottage adjacent to the inn.

The smugglers themselves had fled like the mist into the dawn and the surrounding countryside and mine host himself was safely esconced at the Fishing Boat Inn doubtless thinking himself safe, not so however, the indignant landlord found himself in chains and on his way to trial, the certain shadow of the gallows a constant spectre. The evidence must have been largely circumstantial at best but with no one else in the dock the justices might have been tempted to feel that any available neck should be the one to be stretched, 'Pour encourager les autres'.

It was now and never at a more opportune moment that Isaac discovered an ally in the law — in the excitement of the chase the excisemen had omitted to hoist their colours thus the pursuit was illegal — case dismissed. Free to return and with a greater mystique than before Isaac survived to recount the tale of the fight which no doubt was re-lived many times thereafter in the bar of the Fishing Boat Inn.

The Northumbrian shore stretches like a lonely ribbon weighed at either end by an ancient port. In the earlier part of the medieval period Berwick stood as a rival for size and importance to Newcastle though the holocaust unleashed by Edward Plantagenet destroyed her supremacy for good. As a result of this sudden, violent and enforced decline Newcastle which had in fact, been overshadowed previously by her northern rival prospered and grew.

Despite her growing importance as a mercantile centre Newcastle had severe drawbacks as a naval base — heavy silting in the Tyne estuary blocked the passage for larger warships which then had to anchor off Tynemouth Haven. Against this there were numerous advantages, Newcastle was an impressively walled and well defended city, by far the most secure base on the north-eastern seaboard, there were ample facilities for victualling, skilled mariners for hands, tradesmen for refitting and repairs, shipwrights, carpenters, sailmakers, ropemakers and the like. As a final, major attraction the port owned a goodly number of vessels nearly half of which, by the early sixteenth century were fit for conversion to men-o-war.

The Tudor era was to herald a distinct development in Newcastle's role as a base for offensive naval operations along the Northumbrian and Eastern Scottish coasts. Deteriorating relations with the northern neighbour and an increasing French involvement made the policing of these waters a prime concern. The favoured route for ships from the continent was to make directly for the mouth of the Forth and the sanctuary of Leith Docks. Obviously a squadron based at Newcastle and utilising other coastal anchorages such as Skate Roads off Holy Island could do much to disrupt this traffic and thus deprive the Scots of their invaluable aid from abroad.

Under the virile expansionist policy of Henry VIII, Newcastle, 'The meetest place to mount the sea,' became the base for an English fleet intended to sever the 'French Connection' with Scotland by harrying the traffic around the mouth of the Forth. The first clash was in April 1512 when it was the French in the person of their ambassador La Motte and his squadron who drew first blood capturing several English merchantman, including several from Newcastle. Such temerity could not go unpunished, English men-o-war prowled around the mouth of the estuary until the Frenchmen attempted the return journey and this time it was they who were scattered in ignominious flight leaving one of their number taken. Two of the English vessels present at this engagement were from the port of Tyne, *Elizabeth* and *Trinity*.

The early decades of the sixteenth century were studded with brisk sea-duels and fast pursuit, in 1523 Sir Henry Sherburn was commissioned as Admiral of the North Sea with a squadron of ten ships under his command. To this Newcastle contributed nearly half, the *Jesus, Katherine, Matthew,* and *Mary Katherine.* One, more mundane function of this fleet was to shadow the Icelandic trawlers and protect them and their valuable catch from the predatory attentions of privateers and mercantile raiders, a dull business seldom enlivened by action or hot pursuit. One notable encounter did take place, however, when Sherburn commanding *Matthew* and with *William* engaged a large French man-o-war making for the Forth. The exchange that followed was far from cordial, there were thirty-four casualties on *William* alone and Sherburn himself was amongst the dead of *Matthew.* Though suffering heavy loss and severe mauling the crippled Frenchman still managed to limp into Leith and safety.

Life along the Northumbrian coastline was never without excitement whether from marauding northmen, French privateers or domestic smugglers. Scott, admittedly an arch-romantic pays a fine tribute to the priory of Holy Island in *Marmion* — verse that could be applied almost to the entire Northumbrian shore:

> On the deep walls the heathen Dane
> Had pour'd his impious rage in vain,
> And needful was such strength to these
> Exposed to the tempestuous seas.
> Scourged by the winds eternal sway,
> Open to rovers fierce as they,
> Which could twelve hundred years withstand
> Winds, waves and northern pirates hands.

BIBLIOGRAPHY

Andrews W. (1970) *Bygone Northumberland* Reprint S.R. Publishers
Barber R. (1970) *The Knight & Chivalry* Longmans
Barber R. (1980) *The Reign of Chivalry* David & Charles
Bates C. J. (1895) *The History of Northumberland* Elliot Stock
Borland R. (1910) *Border Raids & Reivers* Glasgow
Brand J. (1789) *The History & Antiquities of the Town & Country of Newcastle Upon Tyne* Newcastle
Brown P. (1934-46) *The Friday Books* 4 vols. J & P Books
Bruce J. C. (1947) *Handbook to the Roman Wall* Newcastle
Caldwell H. (1979) *The Scottish Armoury* Wm. Blackwell
County History Committee (1893-1940) *History of Northumberland* 15 vols.
Fraser G. M. (1971) *The Steel Bonnets* Barrie & Jenkins
Froissart J. *Chronicles* Trans. Berners ed. G. & W. Anderson London 1963
Gillingham J. (1981) *Wars of the Roses* Weidenfield & Nicolson
Graham F. (1976) *The Castles of Northumberland* Frank Graham
Graham F. (1974) *Northumbria's Lordly Strand* Frank Graham
Kemp H. (1975) *The Jacobite Rebellion* Almark
Kightly C. (1975) *Flodden: the Anglo-Scottish War of 1513* Almark
Long B. (1967) *Castles of Northumberland* Harold Hill
Mackie J. D. (1969 ed.) *History of Scotland* Penguin
Mann Sir J. (1960) *Arms & Armour in England* H.M.S.O.
Oakeshott R.E. (1960) *The Archaeology of Weapons* Lutterworth Press
Oakeshott R.E./Treece H. (1963) *Fighting Men* Brockhampton Press
Pevsner N./Richmond I.A. (1957) *The Buildings of England: Northumberland* Penguin
Ridpath G. (1858) *The Border History of England & Scotland* Berwick
Scott W. (1869 ed) *Minstrelsy of The Scottish Border* 3 vols. London
(1985) Lang Syne Publishers *Scottish Battles* Reprint
Seymour W. (1975) *Battles in Britain* 2 vols. Sidgwick & Jackson
Sitwell W. (1927) *The Border* Andrew Reid & Co.
Smurthwaite D. (1984) *The Ordnance Survey Complete Guide to the Battlefields of Britain*
Tomlinson W.W. (1863) *Comprehensive Guide to Northumberland* M. Robinson
Tough D.L.W. (1928) *The Last Years of a Frontier* Clarendon Press
Watts S.J. (1975) *From Border to Middle Shire: Northumberland 1585-1625* Leicester University Press
Wedgewood C.U. (1958) *The Kings War 1641-1647* Collins
Young P./Holmes R. (1974) *The English Civil War* Eyre Methuen

Index